Psalms for Contemplation

Psalms
for
Contemplation

by
Carlos G. Valles, S.J.

A Campion Book

Loyola University Press

Chicago

Loyola University Press
3441 North Ashland Avenue
Chicago, Illinois 60657

All excerpts of the Psalms are reprinted from: *Psalms Anew: In Inclusive Language,* compiled by Nancy Schreck and Maureen Leach (Winona, Minnesota: Saint Mary's Press, 1986). Used by permission of the publisher. All rights reserved.

Library of Congress Cataloging-in-Publication Data

Vālesa, Father, 1925-
    Psalms for contemplation / Carlos G. Valles.
        p.   cm.
                Rev. ed. of: Praying together.
    Includes index.
    ISBN 0-8294-0709-X (alk. paper) : $12.95
    1. Bible. O.T. Psalms—Meditations. I. Vālesa, Father, 1925- Praying together. II. Title.
BS1430.4.V34 1990   90-28647
242'.5—dc20   CIP

Cover design and interior illustrations by Beth Herman Design Associates.

Contents

Book II

Book III

Book IV

Book V

Preface

Praying Today

This is a book of prayers. Of actual prayers to be prayed, of living matter for individual prayer, of practical help for religious contemplation, of concrete prayers for personal or community use. In our prayer life we are always learning, always open to the winds of the Spirit, ready to explore new ways of approaching the unapproachable and expressing the inexpressible. A wise and earnest believer asked Jesus in a burst of charming spontaneity: "Lord, I believe; help my unbelief!" I translate the urgent plea into my own prayer situation and say: "Lord, I know how to pray; teach me how to pray!" Every new help is welcome in the unending endeavor of coming closer to God.

The Psalms are a permanent source of inspired prayer. I have lived with them through years in a stormy relationship of wild enthusiasm, devoted intimacy, scholarly study, temporary estrangement, and fervent rediscovery. For me to write a book on the Psalms was inevitable. The only question in my mind, while the seeds of the future work were growing unattended in the depths of my soul, was what shape the writing would take. I soon knew I could not write a cold commentary, but a personal version of each psalm as it had come to form part of my life through loving recitation in a thousand contexts. When I say "version" I don't mean "translation," but my own reliving of the psalm, expressing in personal idiom the echoes that the original psalm awakes in my sensitivity and my experience. That is the way the Psalms make sense to me, the way I pray them, and the way I set them down here. The words in italics are quotations (according to *Psalms Anew: In Inclusive Language*) from the psalm that is being prayed. In the following text I express in my own words the meaning the psalm has for me today and the feelings it arouses in me. I do that as a gentle invitation to each person to find his or her own psalm in the folds of the old. This is the real sense of this book.

The five books into which the Psalms are traditionally divided to echo the five books of the Pentateuch are marked in the text by a separate page.

The Psalms bring with them a blessing, which I have experienced in my own life and which I fondly hope will be experienced by all those who take this book into their hands for prayerful use: the blessing to become a "new song" in our weary lives. Joyful blessing indeed.

Carlos G. Valles, S.J.
St. Xavier's College
Ahmedabad
India

Acknowledgment

In publishing this American edition of Father Valles's prayerful commentary on the Psalms, the editors chose to utilize inclusive language throughout the author's text and also to address a problem in Bible translation that has resulted in masculine-oriented language. One source of the problem is a bias toward the masculine gender inherent in the English language itself. A second source is the historical situation of ancient patriarchal culture. The result has been an unconscious linguistic sexism, with some restriction or obscuring of the meaning of the original biblical text, including the text of the Psalms.

As a better rendering of the Psalms, and in recognition of the direction taken by recent translators, the text of *Psalms Anew: In Inclusive Language* has been adopted for this edition of *Psalms for Contemplation*. This text, compiled by Nancy Schreck and Maureen Leach and published in 1986, has been made available through the kindness of Saint Mary's Press, Winona, Minnesota.

It should be noted that adoption of *Psalms Anew*—from the Hebrew, not from the Septuagint version—has resulted in a different numbering of the Psalms, usually by one unit, from that encountered in most Catholic editions. Father Valles's text has been modified accordingly.

Joseph F. Downey, S.J.
Editorial Director
Loyola University Press

Book I

Psalm 1

Prayer of the Lucky

Oh, the joys of those who . . . delight in the law of Yahweh.

I am lucky, Lord, and I know it. I am lucky I know you, I know your ways, I know your will, I know your law. Things make sense to me because I know you, because I know there is a purpose behind this difficult world, a loving hand behind my life, a gentle touch in all I do and a constant presence within me day and night. I know my way, because I know you, and you are the Way. And when I think of it, I realize the happiness that is mine for knowing you and living with you.

There is so much confusion all around me, Lord, so much darkness and doubt and sheer bewilderment with life in people I know and in writings I read, that I myself suffer with that suffering and go blind in that darkness. People speak of their aimlessness, their lack of purpose, of direction, and of certainty, their sense of drifting from nowhere to nowhere, their emptiness, their shadows, their void. All touches me, and I too feel it in myself, as brother to my brothers, as sister to my sisters, and as member of my race.

Many people are like *chaff which the wind blows away,* painfully hanging on the whims of the breeze, on the demands of a competitive world and the sudden storms of their own desires. They are unable to steer their own course and define their own lives. This is the disease of modern society, and I learn from your Word that it was also the disease of ancient society when the first psalm was written. I also know your remedy for it: your word, your will, and your law. Faith in you gives direction and purpose and firmness and strength. Only you can steady the hearts of humankind, only you can enlighten their minds and direct their course. Only you can give stability in a changing world.

It is you who give me roots for strength and for life. You make me feel like a tree *planted by streams of water;* I feel the current of your grace running through my soul and my very body, keeping ever green my power to think and my power to love, and turning my desires to fruit when the season comes, and the sun of your presence blesses the crops in the fields that you yourself have sown.

I need security in an insecure world, Lord, and your law, which is your will and your love and your presence, is my security. I thank you, Lord, as the tree thanks the water and the earth.

Psalm 2

I Am Your Child

These are the words I most like to hear from your lips, Lord: "You are my child." It takes faith to proclaim them before my own misery and before a skeptical crowd, but I know they are true, and they are the root of my life and the core of my being. Daily I call you Father, and I call you Father because you have called me child. That is the dearest secret of my life, my most intimate joy, and my deepest claim to happiness. The initiative of your love, the thrill of creation, the intimacy of fatherhood. The loving accent with which I hear you say the words, at once sacred and tender, *"You are mine."*

And I love just as much your next words: *"It is I who have begotten you this day."* I know that for you every moment is today and every instant is eternity. The timelessness of your eternal present is the fullness of your being, and I want to reflect in my fragmented existence the never-fading freshness of your permanent "now." I want to feel that I am your child today, that you are giving me life at every instant, that with you every moment is new and every instant alive, that life begins anew whenever I think of you again, because at that moment you again become my Father.

Keep breathing into me, Father, the newness of the birth you give me day by day, that I may never get tired of living, may never get bored with life, may never get stuck in the dullness of earthly existence. That is a recurring temptation with me, and, I sadly guess, with many people around me too. Life is so repetitive, so monotonous, so gray, that each day looks similar to the previous one, all run to the same timetable, and the routine of a necessary job takes away the joy of living from a day that consists only in getting ready for the office, going there, slogging or idling there, getting back home, and wearily waiting until it is time to go there

5

again the next day. Even my prayers look alike, and, forgive me, but even my encounters with you in contemplation and sacrament are marred on my side by the shadow of previous ones and the formalism of repeated procedures. Teach me your "today" in order to make every moment of my life come alive again.

Since you are my Father you give me *the ends of the earth* for my inheritance. I now know that all is mine because all is yours and because you are my Father. Make me feel at home in every situation and in every circumstance because you are its Master and I am your child. Make me enjoy the earth, explore its riches, and brave its dangers. Make me feel stranger to no one and out of place nowhere. Make me rule the earth, not in power and might, but in the joy of life and peace of heart that come from your presence and attract all your children and make for friendship and nearness and trust among humankind. Make me rule by serving others and loving all in your name. That is how I want to embrace the ends of the earth that you give me for my own.

Yes, I hear the cries and the protests and the turmoil. *The rulers of the earth arise and plot against Yahweh and the Anointed.* People will not keep quiet when someone declares himself or herself a child of God. There is the irony, the scorn, the veiled contempt and the open threats. There is a strange resentment all around when someone finds peace and proclaims joy. The hostile world against the free spirit, the group against the person, the storm against the flower. They vow destruction and plot my ruin. Shall I withstand the onslaught?

But then I hear another voice: your very own. Voice of thunder and power over the tides of humankind. A voice that for me is strength and reassurance because it carries the heavy tone of your seriousness and your anger against the thoughtless mortal who dares to touch those on whom you have set your hand. I hear your laughter peal through the heavens and your blessing riding on it. I am safe in your protection and happy in your keeping. Let the world rage; I am your child. I live now in Zion, *your holy mountain,* and the clouds and the storms cannot shake it and cannot shake me. I keep proclaiming your words, and I keep cherishing being your child. I stand in the shadow of your hands.

Blessed are they who put their trust in God.

Psalm 3

Daily Prayer

Now I can lie down and sleep and then awake, for Yahweh sustains me.

This is my day, Lord, this is my life: the rhythm of my body in tune with the rhythm of your creation, with the stars at night, and with the splendor of your light during the day. I am yours when I work and yours when I sleep; I am yours when I stand erect in the posture that makes me a human being, ready to go and to move and to fight and to look up to heaven; and I am yours when I lie down in the weariness of my body and the confidence of my soul, close to the earth that you have created to hold me in my life and to cradle me in my death, giving shelter to my body as you receive my soul.

Teach me, Lord, the rhythms of your creation, the friendliness with nature, the intimacy with the earth that holds my step and with the air that fills my lungs. Teach me the wisdom of the seasons, the movements of the stars, the ultimate lesson that you always teach me and that I always miss: that in nature as in grace there is rise and fall, there is day and night, there is high tide and low tide, there is joy and there is despondency, there is enthusiasm and there is doubt, there is darkness and there is light.

It takes courage to stand up, and it takes courage to lie down. And, more than that, it takes courage to accept that the whole of life is a succession of getting up and lying down, that the trajectory of living is a wavy line, that I must be ready for the ups and for the downs as they come my way and as I go through them with the sun and the moon and the heavens and the winds. Let me breathe at one with your creation, to fill my body with its life.

From you, Yahweh, deliverance. On your people, blessing!

Psalm 4

Night Prayer

My day comes to an end, a day of labor and joy, of moments of love and moments of anxiety, of impatience and satisfaction. I am going to be myself again for the night, and the last prayer comes to my lips before I close my eyes.

As soon as I lie down, I peacefully go to sleep.

That is my prayer, because that is the wish of my whole being after a day of toil. Sleep is your blessing for the night, as peace is your blessing during the day, and sleep comes where there is peace. You have given me peace among the thousand pressures of the day, among the envy of people, the burden of work, and the perplexity of decisions. *The joy that you give me is much greater than the joy of those who have an abundance of grain and wine*, and the care you have taken of me during the day has prepared me lovingly for the rest in the night.

I know the fears of those in the desert when they laid themselves down to sleep, the ones who made these psalms out of their lives and their experience. I know the fear of the wild beast that may attack at night, of the personal foe who may seek vengeance in the dark, of the enemy tribe that may spring a surprise attack while everyone sleeps. And I know my own fears, too. The fear of a new day, the fear of meeting life again, of facing myself in the uncertain light of a new dawn. The fear of competition, the fear of failure, the fear of not being able to stand the strain to be what I daily have to be, to meet expectations, to play roles, or, harder still, the fear not to be able to ignore those expectations and reject those roles as I know I want to do and don't have the strength to do.

I am afraid of falling asleep thinking that I shall never get up again; and I am afraid of waking up and having to take up again the dreary business of existence. That is the visceral fear that weighs down my life, and its remedy is in you. You watch my sleep, and you protect my steps. Your presence is my sanctuary, your company is my strength. And because I know that, I can now rest with confidence and joy.

As soon as I lie down, I peacefully go to sleep; you alone, my Strength, keep me perfectly safe.

Psalm 5
Morning Prayer

At dawn I will make ready and watch for you. . . . I will worship at your holy Temple in fear of you.

I begin my day facing your temple, facing the sacrament of your presence, the shadow of your throne. I want the first breath of my day to be a feeling of wonder and awe, an act of worship and acknowledgment of your majesty that fills all things and gives life to all beings.

Your temple sanctifies the earth, and the earth, on which you walked one day, sanctifies the entire cosmos of which it is a minimal and privileged part. That is why I want to face in its direction in the morning to set my bearings and fix my balance.

I know that during the day I am going to be engulfed in a tide of work and stress and suspicion and jealousy. I can trust no one and believe no word. Many want my downfall, and a single false step may cause my ruin. *Because of my enemies, guide me in your justice. . . . Their throats are open graves; they flatter with their tongues.* I am no match for their wiles, I am lost in the double-talk people use today: I want to trust all and believe what they say, but I have suffered too much in the past to be able to be naive again. Make people straight with me, Lord. Make me carry with me the shadow of your temple, the sign of your presence, so that people may speak the truth with me, be honest in their dealings, and direct in their speech. This is the blessing I ask for at the dawn of a new day: May all see you in me, that they may deal gently with me.

In the morning you hear my voice.

Psalm 6

Repentance at Night

I cannot sleep tonight. *I flood my bed with tears;* my bed is crumpled with my grief. I am not weeping for fear of humankind or weakness or self-pity. I lie awake at night because I know I have been mean to you, and that thought breaks my heart and defeats my sleep.

I could not imagine, at that unhappy moment in the day when my conscience blacked out and the evil deed was wantonly done, that its shadow was going to grow so fast on me, destroy my mood and ruin my sleep. And I cannot imagine now how I could have forgotten you at that fateful moment, and acted as if you did not exist, as if you were not in my neighbor whom I well knew I was wronging. I did it coldheartedly, as all do in the harsh competition of this ruthless world. I did it and thought I would get away with it.

But with the night the flimsy support of the surrounding hypocrisy faded away, and I was left alone with my conscience and my deed and the tears on my pillow. I am weary with sorrow, and that is not a made-up feeling of repentance but the naked realization that if I have failed you so badly and unexpectedly today, I can do it again any time, any day, and where does that leave me? How can I trust myself any more? How can I say that I love my neighbor if I can hurt him or her so easily? And if I don't love my neighbor, how can I say I love you? And if I cannot say I love you, how can I sleep?

My vigil today is not penance but love; it is not to implore pardon but to create awareness; or rather, yes, it is to implore pardon in the shape of healing, to ask for mercy, the greatest mercy, which is grace not to do it again.

Be gracious to me, for I am weak; heal me, for my heart is troubled. My soul also is sorely troubled. Turn and save my life; deliver me for the sake of your steadfast love. . . . Yahweh has heard the sound of my weeping. Yahweh has heard my supplication and accepts my prayer.

Psalm 7

God Is My Refuge

I call you *my refuge* and *my shield*, and so you are, and I want to understand the ways in which you protect me and shield me. When I call you my refuge, I don't imagine you as a hidden cave in a high mountain range where I run to hide myself from my enemies so that nobody can find me and I feel safe and secure; or again I don't think that when I invoke your help you come to me and put your shield all around me so that nobody can hurt me and I escape unharmed.

You don't protect me from the outside, but from inside me. You don't run to my aid, you are in me. You don't shield me by wrapping me up, but by being me. You are not an astronaut's suit to guarantee my survival in an unfriendly atmosphere, you are my very skin. You protect my body by giving me a healthy organism and protect my soul by strengthening it in your grace. You protect me by being one with me, and that is my strength.

When I meet a difficulty in life and I think of you, that is not to ask you to remove the difficulty but to give me the strength to face it, not to commit you to bring about a particular outcome but to empower me to accept it whatever it may be; not to impose on you my solution but to make me take yours as mine. That is why you are my strength, because you are my being.

You understand me, and my cry to you in a sudden crisis may take any spontaneous shape. I may claim deliverance, I may protest, I may rebel. I may even sound at times exacting and insolent. But you know me well now, and you know how to translate into coherent language the elementary groanings of my troubled spirit under the weight of pain. What I want in every case is you and your presence and your comforting touch on my wounded soul.

You will even hear me at times, perhaps too often in these psalms, refer to other people as my *enemies*. Here again I hope you understand my language and adapt my meaning. I live in a world ruled by competition, where the success of others is a threat to my advancement, where the very existence of millions around me crowds me out of the center of living. Every person in a line ahead of me is an *enemy*, every driver who by a split second steals the parking place from me is an *enemy*, every one of the candidates interviewed for the same job I badly want and sorely need is an *enemy*. Of course they are all my brothers and sisters, and I embrace them and love them before you, and I am ready to help them if the need arises. I do not wish ill to anybody and will never hurt anybody knowingly. Even if I use the language of war, I am at peace with all humanity and accept them all in you.

My only fear is that the competition I suffer may turn unfair, that bribes and tricks and malpractices may rob me of the job or the prize or the advantage I justly deserved, and that context is where the word *enemy* arises and gets into my prayers. And so when I ask for your protection it is precisely protection against the unfair means others may use to put me down, so that I may not fall a victim to them and may not feel the temptation to hate anybody. Protect me in my life, so that the word *enemy* may never come to my lips. Do justice to me that I may believe in humankind. Shelter me from jealousy that I may feel kindly towards all.

I will thank Yahweh for justice; I will sing to the Most High.

Psalm 8

The Prayer of the Heavens

I am in love with nature. I love the heavens and the earth, the rivers and the trees, the mountains and the clouds. I can sit outside time by the side of the sea and watch without end the play of the waters and the shore, an eternal game of chess between white in the crest of the waves and black in the shadows of the rocks on the limitless board of creation itself. I can contemplate the flow of a river and the dancing of the waters and the singing of the stones and the joy of the current as my own joy in the race to the sea. I can sit under a tree and feel its life as my own in the surging sap from hidden roots to waving leaves. I can wander with a cloud, fly with a bird, or just sit with a flower as it sits out its life contented in fragrance and color in the unknown corner of the virgin forest where it grows and it dies.

I feel one with nature . . . because nature is You.

Nature is fresh with your touch, alive with your breath, trembling with the majesty of your presence, and serene with the blessing of your peace. I enjoy a sunrise because it is exclusively yours, and a sunset because no one can set a hand on it. It is your work alone, and its unspoiled freshness brings ever to me the message of your presence. And when your sun goes down and a friendly darkness, which to me is sign and invitation to closeness and intimacy, spreads over your creation, you imprint on the parchment of your heavens the signature of your stars. Do you realize now why I like to look up to the heavens in the night and decipher in love the code of your exclusive handwriting?

I look at your heavens, the work of your hands, the moon and the stars which you created, and I sing to myself with joyful pride: *God, our God, how glorious is your name over all the earth!*

And in the center of that wonder I see myself. *Who are we that you should be mindful of us, that you should care for us?* I am but a spot of dust in a cosmos of light. But in that spot that is me there is another creation more wonderful than the sky and the stars. The marvel of my body, the secret of my cells, the lightning of my nerves, the palace of my heart, the quickening of my soul, the spark of my understanding, the thrill of my feeling, the pillar of my faith, the wonder inside me, and your signature on it too. I smile in recognition when I see you have made me the ruler of creation, inferior only to yourself. I know my smallness and my greatness, my dignity and my nothingness. And knowing both I accept in simplicity the crown of ruler of creation, the one outside me and the one inside me, and I want to enjoy both fully, the rivers and the mountains as well as the feelings and the wit, the conversation of human beings and the silence of the forest, the home and the sky, the friends and the trees, the books and the stars. I want to enjoy everything as I know you want me to enjoy it to the happiness of your heart and the glory of your name.

God, our God, how glorious is your name over all the earth!

Psalms 9 & 10

Prayer of the Oppressed

So shall you be a stronghold for the oppressed, a stronghold in troubled times. Thus shall those who know your name trust in you, for you have not forsaken those who sought you.

I feel comforted when I read those words, and I realize that the concern for the oppressed was already alive in the heart of those who first made and prayed the psalms. The *cry of the afflicted* and the *hope of the poor* ring in your ears ever since the verses of this psalm first sounded in Israel. The prayer "do not forget the poor, O God, the poor commit themselves to you" is the first prayer of your people, and your answer is recorded in this psalm with prompt gratitude: *Yahweh, you will hear the desire of the afflicted; you will strengthen their hearts; you will incline your ear to do justice to the orphan and the oppressed, so that those born of earth may strike terror no more.*

But at the same time, Lord, I feel sad when I realize with unavoidable evidence that the situation that gave rise to that prayer remains in place today, that the oppression of human beings by other human beings has not yet disappeared from the face of the earth, that there is still injustice and inequality and even slavery among the beings you have created to be free. These are old words that are unfortunately also new: *The wicked do not seek you, because of their pride; all their thoughts are, "There is no God." . . . Their mouths are filled with cursing, deceit, and oppression; under their tongues are mischief and fraud. They lurk in ambush in the villages; in hiding places they murder the innocent; their eyes stealthily watch for the helpless. They lie in wait that they may seize the poor.* People are still murdered today; people are still driven from their homes; people still live in fear and in need. Your world is still marred by injustice, and your children suffer destitution, and thoughtful humankind rises again with pain in its heart at the cry of the poor.

The urgency of the cry today is that *the wicked* are not isolated individuals. Oppression does not come from a single person whom authority could easily restrain. Oppression comes often from authority itself, from the group, from the system, from the vested and complex interests that greed and pride and power have woven into society today to the material advantage of a few and the abject dereliction of millions of your children. My prayer is deeper today as my anguish is wider, and I put a new heart into the words that you yourself inspired.

Arise, Yahweh! O God, lift up your hand! Forget not the afflicted! . . . The helpless commit themselves to you, you have been the helper of the orphan. Break the strength of the wicked and evildoer; seek out wickedness till you find none.

Then I think deeper still, and I discover in myself the roots of wickedness. I, too, cause pain and suffering. I sense in myself the hapless kinship with the so-called *wicked*, and I recognize deep within me the same deviations that, when let loose, bring about the misery the world deplores. I feel the tide of passions and greed and jealousy and lust, and I know I cause harm at times to people close to me. So when I pray for liberation I pray for myself too. Free me from the slavery of my impulses and the unfairness of my judgments. Remove from me the desire to dominate, to impose myself on others, to manipulate, and to rule. Still in me the craving for power, the instinct of ambition. Free me truly from all that harms others, that I may help them to be free. Remove the evil in me and then, through me, remove the evil from all those that come my way and whom I can influence in your name, so that we all may give you thanks and praise together.

Be gracious to me, Yahweh; see what I suffer from those who hate me, O you who lift me up from the gates of death, that I may recount all your praises, that in the gates of the city of Zion I may rejoice in your deliverance.

Psalm 11

The Courage to Live

Today I feel again that black mood that steals its way some-times into my heart under cover of night. The desire to run away from it all, to give up on life, to resign from my job as a human being in which I have been such a signal failure. I am just tired, Lord, tired in the inside of my bones, and my only desire is to lie down and let things be. I am tired of fighting, of dreaming, of hoping, of living. Allow me to sit in a corner, and let the world go its way, once I am free forever from my responsibility to do anything about it. Your own psalm says it: *When foundations fall to ruin, what can the virtuous do?*

I don't even feel like praying, like saying anything, like thinking anything at all. Neither do I want today to argue with you, to protest, to get answers to my questions. I simply have no questions, or no heart to ask them or even to think what they are. I only know that my dreams have not worked, that the world has not changed, and that I myself have not changed into the right kind of person I wanted to be. Nothing has worked, and why should I care anymore? I want to quit, I want to give up, I want to step aside and let things pass as they want to pass, without a word from me.

And yet as I speak to you I know that my words mean exactly the opposite of what they say. I am speaking my despair because I want to hope; I am tendering my resignation because I want to keep working. I know I want to stay, and I know I want to fight. My words now are only the blowing up of the cover of my disappointment that had grown thick with overdrawn patience and had to burst once and for all to give way to cleaner feelings and kinder moods. I will not run away. My existence may or may not make any difference to the world, but my place is here and I mean to keep it and defend it and honor it. I will never run away. It is not in my nature, not in my ways, and if I have allowed that foul mood to come over me, and I have allowed myself to express it, that is precisely because I wanted to come out of it, and I knew that the best way to defeat it was to expose it. It takes courage to live, but that courage comes readily when I think of you and look at you by my side.

The psalm begins with the cowardly advice, *Bird, fly back to your mountain!* And it ends with the word of faith: *The upright shall see God's face.* I will not fly away.

Psalm 12

Word of God and Word of Human

I live in a universe of words, and I feel the tedium and the disgust of listening the whole day to words that mean nothing or mean the opposite of what they say, to words that matter and to words that threaten, to words that entice and to words that cheat: the compliment, the excuse, the simulation, and the plain lie. I never know whether I can trust what I hear or believe what I read. I always feel uneasy before the boast of deceitful people that your own psalm has recorded: *"We are strong with our tongues; our lips are our own. Who rules over us?"*

But then I turn to your Word. Your Word is one and firm and eternal and creative. In the pages of your Book, in the silence of my heart, in the songs of your liturgy and in the incarnation of your Son: your Word is one and true and alive. In the contemplation of your Word I rest and refresh myself from the weariness of cowing down under the words of humankind.

The promises of Yahweh are sure, like tried silver, freed from dross, sevenfold refined.

Thank you for the silver, Lord.

Psalm 13

How Long, O Lord?

How long . . . how long . . . how long? The one cry of my thirsting soul. How long still to go, how long to wait, how long to strive? How long till I learn how to pray, how long till I master my temper, how long till I achieve peace, maturity, and grace? I have been so many years at it, Lord, so many efforts, so many retreats, so many resolutions, so many timetables along the way to better myself, to become a genuine help to others, to be one with you. So many dates have passed, and so many occasions have gone by that you will understand if I grow impatient and wonder and question, how long still for me to go?

I am longing for a future date, for a sizable gain, for a final breakthrough. I have heard of "conversion," "illumination," "samadhi," or "satori," which are words people use to describe the experience of finding you or finding themselves, the decisive step that liberates humankind while on this earth, that opens the soul to you and the arms to all people, that makes a person new and whole and free and true. I know that there is a moment of grace in the lives of human beings when the heavens open and a voice is heard and the wings of a dove flutter above, and a whole life is changed, a new vision is open, and humanity goes forward forever in the strength of the Spirit. I am still in the line by the side of the Jordan. *How long, O God? . . . How long?*

And then I hear your answer: Why ask, how long? Don't you realize that I am already with you, that tomorrow is today, that the future is now, that your life is already working, and that my grace is active in you, that the world is redeemed and the Kingdom has come? Grace is the present, and victory is here. Don't dream of future days, enjoy the present morning. Appreciate what you possess, and work with what you have. You are already free; show it to yourself and to the world, and you will have made your contribution today to the freedom of humankind. Learn the secret: to achieve liberation is to know that you are free. My Son has died for your freedom, and I have accepted his death raising him from the dead; if you believe in his death and resurrection, you believe in your own liberation; proclaim your faith by making it show in your life.

Yes, I believe. I have already received the Holy Spirit, and his gifts are with me. I see now that I have to combine in my heart the two living movements of longing and accepting, of thanking the Spirit for his presence and praying daily "Come, Holy Spirit," of prizing what I have and hoping for more, of living the present and welcoming the future, of rejoicing in the fullness I have and foreseeing the new fullness I am to receive, of earth and heaven, of promise and fulfillment, of time and eternity.

You understand my double mood, Lord, my longing and my resting, my satisfaction and my desire, my contentment and my impatience. Indeed, you cause them both, as you want me to ask and to thank, to feel happy with what I have, and to expect even more from you. You will have both my prayers, Lord, as I leave both my moods to play on me.

That is the living lesson I learn in a psalm that begins by crying, *How long?* and ends by reporting, *But I have trusted in your steadfast love; my heart shall rejoice in your salvation. I will sing to you, O God, because you have dealt bountifully with me.* So will I too, Lord, with all my heart.

Psalm 14

Here I Am, O Lord!

Yahweh looks down from heaven to see if there are any who are wise, any who worship God. But they have all gone astray; they are all equally bad. Not one of them does what is right, not a single one.

That image of you, Lord, looking down on the beings you have created and finding no one who sincerely seeks you, touches me. I sense your disappointment and your sadness. You seem to be looking for someone you can trust, someone you can call, someone you can entrust your work to. As humankind goes its godless ways, you want to have at least some people you can use as messengers, as prophets, and as agents of your grace in order to remind your people of your love, to repeat your promises, and to proclaim your law. You are looking all around, and you find no one.

Once you said aloud in Isaiah's hearing, "Whom shall I send? Who will go for me?" He spontaneously answered, "Here I am; send me." And you said there and then, "Go then and tell my people." I am not Isaiah, Lord, but I love you, I have zeal for your glory, and I have heard your words. I take them as a personal invitation to me, I come forward and I offer myself to you. Here I am; send me. I am not worthy, I count for nothing, I can do little. But you are looking for volunteers, and I have stepped forward in confidence.

As you look down from heaven, I look up from earth, and our eyes have met. It is a blessed moment in my life. My mission has begun.

Psalm 15

To Stay Close to God

I want to live close to you, and yet I lose again and again the sense of your presence. I just forget you and can live for hours on end as though you did not exist at all. Times of prayer remind me of your existence, but in between I lose you most of the time. I want to regain your contact, I want to *enter your tent*, to *live on your holy mountain*. Tell me how I can achieve that.

I listen eagerly to your answer, and when you have finished the list of your conditions I realize that I already knew them all, and that they all are one, the one commandment of love and justice and fairness to my fellow human beings. Those *whose way of life is blameless, who always do what is right,* . . . *who do no wrong to friends,* they can dwell on your mountain and enjoy the happiness of your presence.

Once a young man asked you, "What have I to do?" And you answered him, "You know the commandments." Your answer to my question "What have I to do?" is always, "You know it already." Yes, I know, and I know that I know. And I remember your reaction before another inquirer who made the same admission: "Then go and do it, and you will have life."

Let me go and do it. Let me love my neighbor and do justice and speak the truth. Let me be fair and loving and kind. Let me serve your people in your name, with the faith and the motive behind it that by serving your children I will obtain you. By doing good on earth, I will gain admission to *your tent* and *live on your holy mountain*.

Psalm 16

Sincerity with Myself

I say to the Lord: *"You are my God; all the good things I have come from you."* . . . *Those who rush to other gods bring many troubles on themselves. I will not take part in their sacrifices; I will not worship their gods.*

I repeat those words, I tell you and tell people and tell myself that I am truly happy in your service and that I feel sorry for those who follow *other gods*, those who make money or pleasure or fame or success their aim, those who care only for the goods of this world and want only to enjoy earthly pleasures and perishable gains. I will not worship their *gods*.

And yet, in moments of sincerity with myself, I know deep within me that I, too, secretly worship those gods. I also like pleasure and praise and success, and I even envy those who enjoy the goods of this earth that are forbidden me because of my vows. I renew my commitment to you, Lord, but I confess that together with it I still feel in my soul the attraction of material pleasures, the pull of the earth, the hidden regret not to be able to enjoy what others enjoy. I still share, darkly and shyly, in the idolatry of other gods and worship unwittingly at their altars. I still try to find happiness sometimes outside you, however much I know that it can only be found in you.

And so my words today are not a boast but a prayer, not a record of achievement but an appeal for help. Make me truly find my happiness in you, make me be content with my inheritance, happy with my portion, satisfied with my boundaries as you have taught me to say. Make me value the place you have allotted me in your Holy Land, and fill my heart and my life with your love and your service. And then make me experience the truth of the words you put in my mouth as I end this psalm: *Your presence fills me with joy, and your help brings pleasure forever.* So be it, Lord.

Psalm 17

Show Me Your Love!

Demonstrate your great love.

All my prayers are contained in that single prayer. Show me your love, your true love, and make me see how marvelous it can be. You have told me your love page by page, almost line by line in the words of your Book, and there is nothing I like more in this world than to hear you tell me that you love me. I believe your declaration and treasure your words. Keep telling me, as I want to hear again and again that you love me.

But then, Lord, I have to apply human standards, which are the only ones I know, to our relationship, and so I humbly and reverently inform you that down here among human beings we usually say that true love is shown not so much in words as in deeds. So when I ask you to show me your love, I am asking you to do things for me. Do keep telling me that you love me, and at the same time keep doing things for me that show that you love me. Surprise me with your grace and bless me with your help. Bring sudden gifts and unexpected presents. Bring your own presence, which is the greatest gift and the highest blessing, and keep using the mysterious ways you have to make your presence felt. Love is infinitely resourceful, even among us, and knows always how to bring instant happiness with the spontaneous tenderness of a genuine gesture. I will say no more.

My faith once more: *I shall see your face, and be filled, when I awake, with the sight of your glory.*

Psalm 18

The Lord's Thunder

I welcome this psalm, Lord, and what you tell me in it; in fact I needed the reminder, and I need it always, as my very dealings with you bring familiarity, and closeness may overshadow reverence. I value that closeness and familiarity, but I realize the danger that I may slip into overfamiliarity and forget the respect I always owe your majesty. You are Father and friend, but you are also Lord and Master, and I want to keep your two faces before me always. That is why I accept in gratitude today the words that speak of you with majesty.

Then the earth swayed and rocked; the mountains trembled and quaked because you were angry. Smoke went up from your nostrils, and devouring fire from your mouth; glowing coals flamed forth. You bowed the heavens and came down; thick darkness was under your feet. You rode on a cherub and flew; you came swiftly upon the wings of the wind. You made darkness a covering, your canopy, thick clouds dark with water. From the lightning of your presence there broke through your clouds hailstones and coals of fire. You thundered in the heavens, you, the Most High, shouting. And you sent out your arrows and scattered them; you flashed forth lightning and routed them. Then the bed of the sea appeared and the foundations of the world were laid bare at your rebuke, O God, at the blast of the breath of your nostrils.

I bow before you as I accept the unfamiliar image of the lightning and the fire. You sit by my side, and you ride on the clouds; you speak softly, and you thunder; you are loving companion, and you are King of kings. I want to learn reverence and distance to deserve and safeguard intimacy and closeness. I will not take advantage of the privilege you give me to be your friend, will never take you for granted, will not become rude or disrespectful. I worship you as I love you.

What I want is to fuse the two attitudes into one in my soul and to approach you at the same time with intimacy and reverence, with tenderness and awe. I want never to forget, even in the closest moment, that you are my God and never to bypass in the stiffest dignity the mutual informality of real friends. I want to be at home in your palace and in my hut, in your heavens and on my earth. I want to deal with you in dialogue and in silence, in commands and in laughter, in your court and on my playground. And, since we meet more often as lifelong friends, I am happy to meet you today as God and King.

And from today on, another lesson. Whenever the skies over me are visited by a storm, I will think of you. The clouds and the darkness and the thunder and the lightning will draw again your image for me, and I will be silent and bow and worship.

Welcome to the storms in my life.

Psalm 19

Nature and Grace

Nature is reliable. The rising of the sun and the coming of the seasons, the phases of the moon and the surging of the tides, the orbits of the planets and the stations of the stars. Cosmic clockwork of eternal precision. The heavens speak of order and guarantee, of the right to expect today the same timetable as yesterday, and of this year, the spring of every year. The imprint of God is upon his creation, and he is a God of order and reliability, a God who can be trusted in all he does, as we trust that the sun will rise tomorrow.

God can be trusted also in his creation of grace. In his law and in his will and in his love. As the sun rises and the rain falls, as the moon waxes and the pole star keeps its post, so the will of God runs with unerring care the universe of grace in the human heart. *Your law, Yahweh, is perfect. . . . Your rule is to be trusted. . . . Your precepts, Yahweh, are right. . . . Your command is clear. . . . Your decrees are faithful.* It is one and the same divine will that runs the stars of heaven and the human heart. One creation mirrors the other so that when we see God working his beauty in the sky we may allow him to work it also in our own hearts.

Day carries the news to day and night brings the message to night. No speech, no word, no voice is heard; yet their news goes forth through all the earth, their words to the farthest bounds of the world.

That music, that message, that secret wisdom speaks to us too. God will never fail us. That is the secret of the stars. The hand that guides them eternally through their uncharted paths, guides us, too, through the impossible labyrinths of our earthly journey. Look at the heavens and take courage. God is behind his creation.

I listen now to that message, Lord, and take it to heart. Your Son taught us to pray that your will be done on earth as it is in heaven. I see all the heavenly bodies doing your will with ready perfection, and I want for me that readiness in following the paths of your grace. This is the prayer I pray daily, as taught by your Son. I know I have the freedom that the sun and the moon do not have: to choose my direction and stray from your path. So I ask you to handle me gently, to nudge me into position, to nurse me along my orbit. Let me have faith in your holy will, let me feel sure that by following its promptings I am taking my place in the total universe you have created, contributing with my freedom to the beauty of the whole. Let me love your commandments and rejoice at your precepts. Let me worship your law, the one law, which is your wisdom and your power in running your heavens and your earth with single harmony. Let me think of you as I salute the rising sun and thank you as I greet the shadows of the night. Make me feel close to your creation, close to the workings of nature, close to your law. Let me sing your glory in my life in living unison with the song of the heavens.

The heavens proclaim your glory, O God, and the firmament shows forth the work of your hands.

Psalm 20

On Chariots and Horses

I do not underestimate chariots and horses, Lord. I know that those who want to fight need weapons and that those who want to succeed need means. I want to do something for you and for your kingdom; I want to spread your word and share out your grace, and for that, too, I need means, and I propose to use them to the best of my ability. I will harness the communication media; I will study techniques and learn methods; I will use the best of modern means to make you known and your message accepted. The best chariots and the best horses for your army, O Lord!

But while I appreciate human means and get ready to make the best of them, I also say clearly that my trust and my hope are not in them. I will seek efficiency, but efficiency by itself will accomplish nothing for your kingdom. This is a delicate balance I want to achieve in my soul: to be efficient for your sake but to also admit that my efficiency counts for nothing. My horses and chariots will do nothing. It is not in them that I trust.

I trust in you, Lord. You want my efforts, and you will have them, with all my weakness and all my good will in them. But success comes from you, from your power and from your grace, and I want to make that clear before you and before my own soul.

Some boast of chariots and some of horses, but we boast in the name of our God.

Psalm 21

My Heart's Desire

You have granted me my heart's desire.

These are words that bring me joy, O Lord. I know that that is your work, your name, your very essence: You are the one who fulfills the desires of the human heart. You have made that heart, and you alone can satisfy it. What is now consoling for me is to know that you in fact do it.

This sets me thinking in the earnestness of your presence: What, in truth, is my heart's desire? Which are the victories I truly want? Now that I see you ready to grant my desires, I want to search my heart and let the core of my being appear before you, that you may see my genuine longing and grant it in your bounty.

But when I do that I feel the shock of shame vibrate through my body. I look at my desires, and I find them so petty! How could I ask for them now in earnest before you? I want a cheap success, a cowardly escape, a personal gratification. I want security and comfort and respectability. Can I call that *my heart's desire* and place it before you as you lift your hand in gracious bestowal? O no, I cannot do that; I keep my shame and delve deeper into my heart.

As I delve deeper into my heart I am in for another shock. I am formulating now "deeper" desires, and I realize that they are only formal, official, academic. I am asking for "your greater glory," "the liberation of humankind," "the coming of the Kingdom." All that is true and beautiful and necessary, but those words are not mine; those expressions are borrowed. Those desires are certainly mine, but only in as much as they are everybody else's. I understand that for *my heart's desire* you expect and mean something personal, concrete, intimate. Something from me to you. From my heart to your Heart, something in mutual love, sincerity, and trust. I want to search deeper still.

And now for a moment I feel happy. I have suddenly told you with a show of humility and a sense of relief at having found the perfect answer: Lord, I leave it to you. You know what is best for me, you love me and want my happiness, and I trust in you and in your wisdom, and so what you want for me is what I want for myself. That is *my heart's desire*. Grant it, and that will make me happy.

Nice words. But hollow. Neat escape. Plain shirking of my responsibility. You have asked me what I want, and I, in cowardly compliment, return the question to you and place on you the burden of the choice. I am covering the shame of my indecision with the gesture of my surrender. Forgive me, Lord. I have not yet found *my heart's desire*.

While I search, I will ask for a grace, as you are still waiting: Give me the grace to know what I really want.

That is now *my heart's desire*.

Psalm 22

When Depression Strikes

I am on my knees as I begin this psalm. It is your psalm, Lord. You said it on the cross, at the height of your agony, when the suffering of your soul brought to a climax the suffering of your body in utter dereliction. *My God, my God, why have you deserted me?*

Those are your words. How can I make them mine? How can I equate my sufferings to yours? How can I climb your cross and utter your cry, forever consecrated by the uniqueness of your passion? I feel that this psalm is yours, and to you it should be left as memorial of your passion, as wounded expression of your personal anguish, as piercing witness of your encounter with death in your body and in your soul. These words belong to Good Friday, to your passion, to you.

And yet I feel that this psalm is also mine, that there are also moments in my life when I, too, have a right and a need to utter those words in humble echo of your own words. I also encounter death, once in my body at the end of my life and many times in the desolation of my soul as I wander through the shadows of this world. I am not comparing myself to you, Lord, but I also know anguish and despair, I also feel loneliness and abandonment. I also have felt let down by the Father, and the words have formed on my parched lips: *My God, my God, why have you deserted me?*

When depression strikes, it makes all people equal. Life loses its meaning; nothing makes sense; every taste is bitter and every color black. There is no point in living. The eye sees no way, and the feet are heavy with inertia. Why eat, why breathe, why live? The bottom of the pit is the same for all people, and those who have reached it, know it. I know my depressions, and I know that they are death in a living body. Utter dereliction. Limit of endurance. Boundary of despair. Suffering makes all people equal, and suffering of the mind in its abjection is the worst suffering. I know its blackness.

Where are you then? Where are you when the black night descends upon my soul? *I call all day, my God, but you never answer; all night long I call and cannot rest.* Indeed, it is your absence that makes up my suffering. If you were by my side, I could bear any hardship, brave any storm. But you have abandoned me, and that is my plight. The loneliness of the cross on Good Friday.

People speak to me then about you. They mean well, but they only sharpen my agony. If you are there, why do you not help me? If you have rescued my ancestors in the past, why do you not rescue me now? *Yet, Holy One, you who make your home in the praises of Israel—in you our ancestors put their trust; they trusted and you rescued them. They called to you and were saved; they never trusted you in vain. Yet here I am.*

I seem to count for nothing before you. I am *more worm than human,* or so I feel just now. *I am like water draining away, my bones are all disjointed, and my heart is like wax melting inside me. My throat is drier than baked clay and my tongue sticks to my mouth. A pack of dogs surrounds me; a gang of villains closes in on me. They tie me hand and foot and leave me lying in the dust of death.*

I had to reach the end of my misery in order to realize that my salvation is only in you. My complaint to you was in itself a hidden act of faith in you. I complained to you that you had abandoned me precisely because I knew you were there. Show now yourself, Lord. Extend your arm, and dispel the darkness that envelops me. Bring back hope to my soul and strength to my body. Put an end to my depression, and let me be a person with joy and faith and zest for life. Let me be myself again and feel your presence and sing your praise. This is passing from death to life, and I want to bear witness to your power to raise my soul from despair as a token of your power to raise humankind into eternal life. You have given me new life, Lord, and I will gladly proclaim your might before my sisters and brothers.

We will proclaim you to generations still to come, your righteousness to a people yet unborn. All this Yahweh has done.

Psalm 23

Joyful and Carefree

I have watched flocks of sheep on green mountain sides. They romp about, they graze at will, they loiter in the shade. They have no sense of hurry, no agitation, no worry. They don't even look at their shepherd; they know he is there and he cares. And so they are free to enjoy the green pastures and the running spring. Happiness under the sky.

Joyful and carefree. The sheep don't calculate. How much time left? Where shall we go tomorrow? Will the rains be enough to provide pastures for next year? The sheep don't care, because there is someone else who cares for them. They live from day to day, from hour to hour. And that is happiness.

Yahweh, you are my shepherd. If only I believe in that, my life will change. My anxiety will go, my complexes will dissolve, and peace will return to my troubled nerves. I will be able to live from day to day, from hour to hour, because he is there. The Lord of the birds in the sky and the lilies of the field. The Shepherd of his sheep. If I truly believe in him I am free to move and to breathe and to live. Free to enjoy life. Every moment is precious because it is unstained with the worry of the next one. The shepherd knows, and that is enough for me. Happiness under grace.

How great is the blessing of believing in Providence. The blessing of living under obedience. The blessing of following the promptings of the Spirit in the paths of life. *Yahweh, you are my shepherd; I shall not want.*

Psalm 24

Lift Up Your Heads!

The world and all that is in it belong to Yahweh, the earth and all who live on it. . . . Who has the right to climb Yahweh's mountain? Or stand in this holy place?

Your majesty fills me with reverence, Lord, and when I think of it I sense my smallness and feel the burden of my unworthiness. Who am I to appear before you, to claim your attention, to engage your love? Let me keep my distance and know my place. Far from me is your holy mountain, your sacred intimacy. It is enough for me to contemplate from afar the summit in the clouds, as your people in the desert contemplated Mount Sinai without daring to approach it.

But as I think of your people in the Old Testament I think also of your people in the New. The memory of Sinai brings to my mind the reality of Bethlehem. The people who feared to approach their God find that their God has come to them. No more fire and lightning. No more clouds round the summit. A cave in the fields and a crib and a baby, and a mother's smile as she cradles him in her arms. God has come to his people.

You have come to me. The supreme gift of personal intimacy. You walk by my side, you hold my hand, you let me recline my head on your breast. The miracle of closeness, the thrill of friendship, the consecration of unity. I cannot let my unworthiness, my shyness, my laziness come between you and me. I want to learn the delicate and privileged art of living close to you.

That is why I need faith, courage, and magnanimity. I need the admonition of your psalm: *Fling wide the gates, open the ancient doors, and the Holy One will come in!* I want to open wide the doors of my heart so that you may come in with the fullness of your presence. No more false humility, no hidden fears, no polite delays. The prince of glory is standing at the gate. The king is asking for friendship. God himself is knocking at my door. For me it is a call to generosity, to confidence, to surrender. A call to open the gates of my soul and receive the divine guest.

Teach me, Lord, how to deal with you. Teach me how to combine intimacy with reverence, friendship with worship, and closeness with awe. Teach me how to lift my head and open my heart as I bend my knee and lower my sight. Teach me never to lose sight of your majesty and never to underestimate your companionship. Teach me your Incarnation. God and human being. Lord and friend. Prince and comrade.

Welcome to the King of glory.

Psalm 25

Do Not Let Me Down

O my God, in you I trust. Let me not be put to shame.

Do you realize, Lord, what will happen to you if you let me down and put me to shame? Somehow I bear your name, and I represent you before your people, so that if my name suffers, your name also will suffer together with mine. We are linked together. My shame, rightly or wrongly, will reflect on you. For the sake of your name, Lord, do not let me down.

I have told others that you are the one who never lets anyone down. What will they say if they see now that you do that to me? I have proclaimed with confidence: Jesus never fails! And are you now going to fail me? That will silence my tongue and cancel my witness. That will try my faith and hurt my friends. That will hinder your kingdom in me. Do not let that happen, Lord.

I know that my sins get in the way. That is why I pray: *Remember not the sins of my youth, or my transgressions; according to your steadfast love remember me, because of your goodness, Yahweh! . . . For your name's sake, O Yahweh, pardon my guilt, for it is great.* Don't look at my wrongdoings but at my trust in you. On that trust I base my whole life. On that trust I speak and I act and I live. This trust that you will never fail me. That is my faith, and that is my boast. You never fail. You will not make me lose face. You will not let me down.

At times when I am under a cloud and see no light and can expect no deliverance, it is hard to say that. I know that you work at long range, and my short patience demands an immediate release when you would rather contemplate a long-term plan. We follow different timetables, and my shortsightedness does not easily fit into your eternity. I am ready to wait, ready to keep your time and to follow your step. But do not forget me in the end,

Lord. Let my trust come through and my hope be redeemed. Give me signs of your favor that my faith may be strengthened and my boast be upheld. Show me in my life how you never let down those who trust in you, that I may continue to feel that confidence and to proclaim that joy. The Lord never lets down his people.

Let none that wait for you be put to shame.

Psalm 26
Prayer of the Upright

I would not have dared to pray this psalm, Lord, but I am grateful you offer it to me and invite me to make it my own. A psalm of innocence and sincerity; the prayer of the upright and blameless soul. That is not exactly me. I know my failings and regret my shortcomings. I hurt people; I court praise; I seek pleasure; I am not true to myself. There are black moments in my life and dark corners in my conscience. I am not innocent and pure. I cannot stand before you and claim righteousness.

And yet that is what you are inviting me to do, and I secretly rejoice, almost against myself, when I hear your invitation and get ready to answer it. I know I have done wrong things, but in my heart of hearts I worship truth, and I wish all people well. I do not act out of malice; I do not wish to hurt; I do not mean to disobey. I am weak, yes, but not wicked. I love goodness and cherish honesty. I would like all to be happy and the whole world to be at peace. There is goodness in me, and that is the deepest layer of my being. I want to feel good, and so I welcome your invitation to say the prayer of the just person.

Do me justice, O God, for I have walked in integrity, and in you I trust without wavering. Search me, O God, and try me; test my soul and my heart. For your love is before my eyes, and I walk in your truth. . . . I wash my hands in innocence, and I process around your altar. . . . But I walk in integrity; redeem me and have pity on me.

That is me at my best. And I feel happy to appear before you, Lord, for once in that light. I am happy to stand up with the confidence you have won for me, to lift up my face, to smile in innocence and to speak in freedom. Yes, I am your child, and in asking your blessings I am asking for justice. You have given me the right to speak so, and I claim it with simplicity. I ask for justice.

I am asking for your blessing and my inheritance. I am asking for peace and for joy. I want to feel that I am a faithful child to you and a good person to all. This I call justice, and this is what I expect from you.

Do me justice, O God, for I have walked in integrity.

Psalm 27

I Seek Your Face

This is the one longing of my life that sums up all my other longings: to see your face. These are bold words that I would not presume to utter if you had not given them to me. In the old days nobody could see your face and live. Now you remove the veil and uncover the presence. Once I know it, what else can I do but to seek that face and long for that presence? This is now my one desire, the aim of all my actions and the very meaning of my life.

One thing have I asked of you, Yahweh, this I seek: to dwell in your house all the days of my life, to behold your beauty and to contemplate on your Temple. . . . My heart says to you, "Your face I do seek."

I know your word, and I know your precepts. I know what wise and holy people say about you, what your saints have taught and your friends have revealed of their dealings with you. I have read many beautiful books and taken part in fruitful discussions about who you are and what you do and why and when and in which way. I have even passed examinations with you as a subject, though I sometimes wonder what marks you would have given me if you had been on the board of examiners. I know a good deal about you, and I even used to believe that that was enough, and that that was all that could be expected of me in the darkness of this transitory existence.

But now I want more, because I know it is possible and you want it and are calling me to attain it. I want to see your face. I have knowledge, but I now want experience; I have your word, but I now want your face. I have secondhand references, and now I aspire to direct contact. It is your face, O Lord, that I seek. Nothing else will satisfy me.

You know your times, and you know your ways. You have the power, and you have the means. You are the Lord of the human heart, and you can enter it at will. Now you have my invitation and my petition. It is for me to wait with patience, with longing, and with love. That I will do with all my heart.

Wait for Yahweh; be strong, and let your heart take courage. Yes, wait for God!

Psalm 28

Rock of Ages

You are my Rock. In a world where everything changes, where human beings are fickle and their moods like feathers in the wind, where nothing is stable, nothing permanent, nothing reliable; in a world of insecurity and instability you are my Rock.

You stand while everything falters. You are firm, steady, eternal. You alone offer security and safety. In you alone can I rest and take refuge and feel at peace. You are my Rock.

Round me there are quicksands and marshes and slippery paths and shaky ground. I must be slow and cautious. I cannot run and jump and dance at will. I must mind every step and test every stone. There is painful progress and constant apprehension on the grounds of life. There is no one I can really trust; nothing I can safely rely upon. There is always doubt and suspicion and fear. When everything is unsteady, the mind itself is restless, and peace flies from the soul.

That I myself am not steady is my greatest trial. I am a bundle of doubts. It is not only that I don't trust anybody, but that I don't trust myself. I waver and hesitate and stumble. I don't know what I want and am not sure where I want to go. Uncertainty is not only outside me, but inside me, very much inside me, in my decisions and my opinions and my beliefs. I take a hundred resolutions and fulfill none; I start on a hundred journeys and reach the end of none. I am a reed shaken by the wind. I lack firmness, and I need desperately someone I can lean on.

And that is you, Lord. You are my Rock. The firmness of your word, the uniqueness of your truth, the permanence of your eternity. You are the Rock jutting out in the midst of waves and sands and winds and storms. Just to look at you gives me repose, and to know that you are there and that I can rest in you gives me stability. With you I feel the unshakable presence of an incarnation in stone. I lean against your slope, safe and secure. In a world of changes, you are my Rock, Lord, and that very thought gives peace to my soul.

To you, Yahweh, I call; my Rock, hear me. . . . You are my strength and my shield. In you my heart trusts and I find help; then my heart rejoices, and I praise you with my song. You are the strength of your people, the stronghold where your anointed find salvation.

Psalm 29

Darkness in the Sky

The sky is dark, the storm is raging, the forces of evil seem to have taken hold of heaven and earth. The storm is confusion and destruction; in it there is danger and death. Humanity is afraid of the storm and runs for cover when lightning strikes. Humanity cowers under the powers of darkness.

And yet you teach me now, Lord, that you ride on the storm. You are in it; you make it; you direct it. You are the Lord of the storm. You are in the darkness as you are in the light; you reign on the clouds as you reign in the blue sky. Thunder is your voice, and lightning is the trace of your finger. I must see your presence in the thick of the storm as I see it in the sunshine. I worship your coming as the Lord of nature.

The God of glory thunders upon many waters. The voice of God is powerful; the voice of Yahweh is full of majesty. The voice of Yahweh breaks the cedars, breaks the cedars of Lebanon. . . . The voice of Yahweh flashes forth flames of fire.

After I recognize you in the storms of nature, I learn to recognize you in the storms of my own soul, when my own sky grows dark and my horizons tremble and the lightning of despair strikes the wilderness of my heart. If blessings come from you, trials also do. If you are sun, you are also thunder, and if you bring peace you bring also the sword. You come in consolation and in temptation alike. Yours is the day, and yours is the night, and I want to accept you now also as Lord of the night in my own life.

I even sense you closer now in the storm, Lord, than in the calm. When things go well and life is normal, I take you for granted; I minimize your role in my life; I forget you. When darkness comes and imposes on me the sense of my own frailness, I think of you, and I take refuge in you. I accept the mystery of the storm, the trial by thunder and lightning. I feel close to you in my dark hours, and I bow before your majesty in the storms that rage through the landscape of my soul. You are the Lord of the storm; you are the Lord of my life.

Yahweh sits enthroned over the flood; God sits enthroned forever. May Yahweh give strength to the people, blessing the people with peace!

Psalm 30

Moods of the Soul

I want to uncover the moods of my soul before myself and before you, Lord. I want to know how to deal with myself when I am high and when I am low, to handle my optimism and my pessimism, to learn how to react to spiritual joy and to human dejection; and, above all, I want to learn how to ride the tides of feelings, the changes of mood, the sudden storm and the unexpected bliss, the darkness and the light, and the uncertainty that never allows me to know how long a mood will last and when the opposite mood will strike.

I am at the mercy of my moods. When I feel joyful, everything looks easy, virtue is obvious, love is spontaneous, and a firm assurance grows on me that this is the way it will be with me from now on and forever. Yes, I tell myself, I have finally arrived; I have matured in my spiritual life; I have myself well in hand; I have gone through ups and downs, and I know there will still be small changes and variations, but fundamentally I know now what to expect. I am well established, and nothing will seriously shake me now. I am an old-timer in the ways of the spirit, and I know perfectly well where I stand. Through God's grace I am firm and steady.

You know me well, Lord, and you yourself put those words on my lips when you invite me to recite this psalm: *I felt secure and said to myself, "I will never be defeated."* That was my unwarranted confidence, my immature boast. I really thought I could never be shaken now.

And then your psalm continued as my life continues: *When you hid yourself from me, I was filled with fear.* I was shaken again to my very foundations, and then my despair was as total and absolute as my boast had been before. I am good for nothing; I shall never learn; I am now, after so many years, right where I was at the beginning of my spiritual life. I don't know how to pray, how to keep peace in my soul, how to deal with God. I don't know, and I'll never learn now; I can just as well give up and resign myself to a low and humdrum existence. The stars are not for me.

When I am down, I forget that I ever was up and think I shall never be up again, and when I am up and high, I persuade myself that that is the way it will always be and that there is nothing to fear any more. My memory is short, and so my suffering is long. I am the slave of my moods, the plaything of the breeze that blows on my soul. I am hot when it is hot, and I am cold when it is cold. I lack the persevering steadfastness of the seasoned worker, the proven seeker. I waver and stumble and fall. I want a greater balance for my life, a larger perspective, a truer patience. I want for me the long-term view that experience in your ways gives to those who know and trust you.

For this I pray: that when I am in high spirits, I may remember that I was low before, and that when I am low, I may trust that the high spirits will come again. Then truly *I will give thanks to you forever.*

Psalm 31

My Life in Your Hands

I feel happy while I say those words: *In you, Yahweh, I trust; I say, "You are my God." My fate is in your hand.* A sense of relief sweeps over me, a feeling of satisfaction and safety in the midst of a troubled world. *My fate is in your hand.* Whatever happens to me, whatever life brings to me, whatever winds blow and waters flow on the fields of my life, all that is in your loving hands. I need no more.

My fate, my fortunes. Good fortune and bad fortune, things I like and things I dislike, occasions I look forward to and occasions I fear, pleasure and pain, joy and sorrow. All that is in my life, and all that is in your hand. You know the time; you know the measure; you know my strength and my lack of it; you know my longings and my limitations, my dreams and my realities. All that is in your hand, and you love me and want the best for me. My best fortune is to know that my fortunes are in your hands.

Let that faith grow in me, Lord, and put an end to worry in my life. I surely will continue to work for my fortunes; I am too much of an achiever and a compulsive worker to let go of things and lower my efforts. I will continue to work, but with a happy face and a light heart because my fortunes are in your hand. I can look up and smile and sing because now the burden is light, and the yoke is easy. My effort will be the same, but now I know that the result is in your hand and, therefore, out of my own hands and out of my mind. Peace has come to my heart because *"You are my God." My fate is in your hand.*

Psalm 32

Shadows in My Soul

I have done wrong, and I have tried to forget it, to play it down, to hush it up, to put it out of my mind. I secretly justified myself before my own conscience: This is nothing big after all; they all do it anyway; I was helpless, and what else could I have done? Let us forget it, and the memory of it will pass away, the sooner the better.

But the memory did not pass away. I felt sad and disturbed. The more time passed, the sharper the pang in my conscience became. My attempt at hiding from myself my own wrongdoing succeeded only in making me feel unhappy and miserable.

As long as I would not speak, my bones wasted away with groaning all day long. . . . My strength was dried up as by the summer's heat.

I was dissatisfied with myself and angry at my own weakness. There was something hanging in my past, an unhealed wound, an unfinished chapter, an unallayed guilt. I had swallowed poison, and it was still in me spreading its baleful influence to my whole organism in despondency and frustration. I could bear it no longer.

Then I acknowledged my sin to you, and did not cover my guilt. I said, "I confess my faults to you."

I made a clean breast of it before myself and before you, Lord. I accepted my responsibility, I owned up, I confessed. And at once I felt on me the favor of your countenance, the touch of your healing, the relief of your pardon. And I exclaimed in my new joy: *Happy are those whose fault is taken away, whose sin is covered. Happy those whose sin Yahweh does not count, in whose spirit there is no guile.*

I want from you, Lord, the grace of transparency. I want to be transparent to myself and to you, and so to all men and women with whom I deal. To have nothing to hide, nothing to disguise, nothing to gloss over in my behavior and in my thoughts. I want to put an end to the shadows in my soul or, rather, to accept them as shadows, to own them, to take myself as I am, dark spots and all, and as such appear before my own gaze and that of all people and that of your own majesty, my Judge and my Lord. Let me know myself, and let others know me as I am. Let me be honest, sincere, and candid. Let me be transparent in my lights and shadows, and the blessing of reality will offset in me the stain of fallibility.

Happy are those . . . in whose spirit there is no guile.

Psalm 33

The Lord's Own Plans

The Creator frustrates the plans of the nations, overthrows the designs of the peoples. The Creator's own designs shall last forever, the plans of God's heart for all ages.

These are words of reassurance to me, Lord, and to all those who wish humankind well and are concerned about its future. I read the papers and listen to the radio and watch television, and I see the news that darken humankind's existence from day to day. *The plans of the nations.* All is violence and ambition and war. Nations plan how to conquer other nations, and human beings plan how to murder other human beings. Every new weapon produced in the armament race is present witness and potential instrument of the black thoughts that people entertain today all over the world, of *the plans of the nations* to destroy each other. Mistrust, mutual threats, spying, blackmailing. The universal nightmare of the international power struggle that threatens the very existence and continuation of humankind.

Before that brutal evidence of worldwide violence good people feel the frustration of their helplessness, the uselessness of their efforts, the defeat of good sense, and the flight of sanity from the international scene. *The plans of the nations* spell misery and destruction for those very nations, and nothing and nobody seems to be able to stop that insane race to self-annihilation. More even than worry for the future, what harasses the mind of thinking people today is the sorrow and surprise at the foolishness of humankind and the inability to make others see reason for their own good. When will that madness stop?

The Creator frustrates the plans of the nations. That is the assurance and that is the hope. You will not allow, Lord, humankind to destroy itself. When I think of it, those words, those *plans of the nations* referred to a situation of many centuries ago when the nations around Israel plotted against it and against one another for mutual destruction, but those plans were brought to nothing. Humankind is still alive. History continues. In that history the plans of destruction still continue, but then the watch of the Lord also continues and holds back the hand of destruction from the face of the earth. The future of humankind is safe in his hands.

Against *the plans of the nations* stand now *the Creator's own designs*, and that is the greatest consolation of believing people in their thoughts and care for their own race. We don't know those plans, and we don't ask to be told about them, since we trust the Planner, and it is enough for us to know that the plans exist. Being the Lord's plans they will be beneficial to humankind, and they will be unfailing in their execution. Those plans will safeguard each nation and defend each individual in ways he or she does not know now but will learn one day in the joy and the glory of the Lord's salvation. The Lord's victory will in the end be humankind's victory and the victory of every nation that puts its trust in him. His plans are the beginning on earth of a blissful eternity.

The Creator's own designs shall last forever, the plans of God's heart for all ages. Humankind's history is in the hands of the Lord.

Psalm 34

Taste and See

I let the words sound in my ears: *O taste and see that Yahweh is good. Taste and see.* That is the most loving and the most serious invitation I have received in my life: to *taste and see* the Lord's goodness. It goes beyond study and knowledge, beyond reasoning and discourse, beyond learned books and holy Scriptures. It is personal and direct, concrete and intimate. It speaks of contact, presence, experience. Not just "read and reflect" or "listen and understand" or "meditate and contemplate," but *taste and see.* Open your eyes and stretch out your hand; awaken your senses and sharpen your feelings; bring out the most intimate power of your soul in spontaneous reaction and personal depth; exercise your power to sense, to feel, to *taste* what is good and beautiful and true. Let it play joyfully and lovingly on the ultimate goodness and beauty and truth; the goodness, beauty, and truth of the Lord himself.

Taste is a mystical word, and now it is mine by right. I am a mystic by vocation. I am called to *taste and see.* No shyness will keep me back; no false humility will make me withdraw. I am grateful and courageous and want to respond to the divine invitation with all my being and with all my joy. I will open myself to the intimate delights of the presence of God in my soul. I will treasure the secret exchange of trust and love beyond words and beyond description. I will enjoy without measure the final communion of my soul with its Creator. He knows how to make his presence felt and how to take in his close embrace the souls he has created. It is for me to accept and to surrender in grateful wonder and silent bliss, to welcome the touch of God upon my soul.

I know that in order to awaken my spiritual senses I have to still my intellect. Too much reasoning blinds intuition, and human cleverness hinders divine wisdom. Let me learn to be quiet, to be humble, to be simple. Let me transcend for a while all that I have studied and all that I have learned; let me stand before God in the nakedness of my being and the humility of my ignorance. Only then will he fill my emptiness with his fullness and redeem my nothingness with the totality of his being. To taste the sweetness of the divinity I must purify my senses from the encumbrance of past experience and inborn prejudice. I must become a virgin slate before the new light, a soul before the Lord.

The object of the sense of taste is the fruits of the earth or the fruits of the Spirit: "love, joy, peace, patience, kindness, generosity, faithfulness, gentleness, and self-control" (Galatians 5:22).[1] These fruits are a divine harvest in human hearts, and this harvest we are called to reap and taste and enjoy and assimilate so that joy may burst into our lives, as the crops of the season ripen on the fields of humankind, and so that the praise of the Lord may resound till the ends of the earth.

I will bless Yahweh at all times; praise shall continually be in my mouth. . . . Glorify Yahweh with me and let us exalt God's name together.

---

[1] New Revised Standard Version (Grand Rapids, Mich.: Zondervan Bible Publishers, 1989), 948.

Psalm 35

"I Am Your Salvation"

Say to my soul, "I am your salvation."

I know that you are my salvation, Lord; but now I want to hear it from your own lips. I want the sound of your voice, the firmness of your gesture. Let me hear you directly and personally, addressing me in my own heart. Let me receive from you the message of hope and redemption for my life: *I am your salvation.*

And once I have received from you the message of salvation, I trust I will see it carried out in the trying vicissitudes of my daily life. You are always with me, and you are my salvation, so that now I can expect this salvation to work its wonders for me day to day as I need your help, your guidance, and your strength. If you are truly my salvation, make me feel it effectively in the daily difficulties that beset me.

In particular, Lord, save me from the people who wish me ill. There are such people around me, and the burden of their jealousy bears down heavily upon my powers of endurance. There are people who rejoice when I encounter misfortune and who laugh when I fall.

Gathering together, they are happy now that I have fallen. They mock me. Complete strangers rip me to pieces with shouts, ridiculing me with their taunts, grinding their teeth at me. Yahweh, how much longer will you allow this? . . . Do not let my lying enemies gloat over me; prevent the sly glances of those who hate me for no reason.

I do not mean to complain about anybody, Lord; they know their intentions and they handle their consciences; but I do feel at times the friction, the tension, the enmity that harden faces and strain relationships. I want to look on everybody as a friend, and on every co-worker as a partner, but I find that difficult in a world of competition and backbiting and jealousy. What I want is for me to accept everybody personally, so that by my acceptance of others they may come, in turn, to soften their stand and to accept me. Remove all bitterness from my heart, and make me kind and gentle in order to invite kindness and gentleness from others and to clear the air wherever I live and wherever I work. Be my salvation by redeeming me and all those I live with and deal with from the blight of jealousy. Let us all rejoice at the good that each of us does. Let us consider as our own achievement whatever our brother or sister has achieved.

Then my soul will celebrate the Most High, rejoice that God has saved me.

Psalm 36

The Fountain of Life

You are the source of life, and in your light we see light.
I want to be alive, to feel alive, to sense the energies of creation surge through all the cells of my body and all the tissues of my soul. Life is the essence of all blessings from God to humankind, the touch of God's right hand that makes a lump of clay into a living being and converts a dormant shape into the king of creation. Life is the glory of God made movement and growth, the divine Word translated into laughter and speech, the eternal love throbbing in the human heart. Life is all that is good and vibrant and joyful. Death is the end of all.

I want life for me, for my thoughts and for my feelings, for my encounters and my conversations, for my friendship and for my love. I want the spark of life to kindle all that I do and think and am. I want my step to be quickened, my thought to be sharpened, my smile to be lit by the breaking through of the life from within me. I want to be alive.

And you are the fountain of life. The closer I am to you, the fuller I am with life. The only life is the one that comes from you, and the only way to share it is to be close to you. Let me drink from that fountain; let me sink my hands in it to feel its freshness and its purity and its strength. Let the living waters of that fountain flow through me to vivify me with the play of its waves upon my heart.

You are also the light. In a world of darkness, of doubt, and of uncertainty, you are the pointing ray, the welcome dawn, the revealing noon. Again, to see I have only to be close to you. *In your light we see light.* I want your light, your vision, your point of view. I want to see things the way you see them; I want your perspective, your horizon, your angle on persons and events and the history of humanity and the vicissitudes of my life. I want to see things in your light.

Your light is the gift of faith. Your life is the gift of grace. Give me your grace and your faith that I may see and live the fullness of your creation with the fullness of my being.

Your love, Yahweh, reaches to heaven; your faithfulness to the skies. Your justice is like a mountain—your judgments like the deep. To all creation you give protection. Your people find refuge in the shelter of your wings. They feast on the riches of your house; they drink from the stream of your delight.

Lord, give me to drink.

Psalm 37

Wait for the Lord

Trust in Yahweh and do good so you will dwell in the land and enjoy security. Take delight in Yahweh, who will give you the desires of your heart. Commit your way to Yahweh; trust in God who will act, bringing forth your vindication as the light, and your right as the noonday sun. Be still before Yahweh, and wait patiently; fret not over those who prosper, over those who carry out evil. Refrain from anger and forsake wrath! . . . For the wicked shall be cut off, but those who wait for Yahweh shall possess the land.

I need those words: "Wait patiently for the Lord." I am all impatience and hurry and hustle and bustle, and I don't know any more whether that movement is holy zeal or just ill temper. It is all for your Kingdom, of course, for the good of my soul and the service of my neighbor, but there is, through it all, a sense of inner pressure as though the welfare of humankind depended entirely on me and my efforts. I want to do, to achieve, to bless, to heal, to set right all the evils of the world, beginning, of course, with all the shortcomings of my humble person, and so I have to act, to pray, to plan, to organize, to conquer, to achieve. There is too much activity in my little world; there are too many ideas in my head and too many projects in my hands. And in the middle of my mad rush I hear that single word from on high: Wait.

Wait.

Wait patiently for the Lord.

All my duties, all my obligations, all my plans, all my work are in that simple word. Wait. Keep quiet. Don't run about. Don't fuss; don't fret; don't drive yourself hard and everybody else harder still. Don't behave as though the whole delicate balance of the cosmos depended every moment on you. Wait and be still. Nature knows how to wait, and its fruits come in due season. The earth waits for the yearly rain; the fields wait for the seeds and the crops; the tree waits for the spring; the tides wait for their appointed time in the heavens, and the burning stars wait ages and ages for the eye of humanity to discover them and think of the hand that placed them in their orbits. All creation knows how to wait for the fullness of time that gives it meaning and gathers the harvest of hope into handfuls of joy. Only human beings are impatient and burn their time. Only I still need to learn the heavenly patience that brings peace to the mind and lets God be free to act at his own time and in his own way. The secret of Christian action is not to do but to let God do. *Trust in God who will act.*

If I only would let you do in my life and in my world what you want to do! If I only would learn not to interfere, not to be anxious, not to fear that all will be lost if I don't keep things tight in hand! If I only had faith and trusted you and let things go to you and let you come when you want and do what you please! If only I would learn how to wait! Waiting is believing, and waiting is loving. Waiting for the coming of Christ is anticipating his coming in the private eschatology of one's own heart. Blessed are those who wait, because the joy of meeting will crown the faithfulness of waiting.

Psalm 38
Prayer of the Sick

Sickness has struck me, and I have lost my courage. So long as my body was feeling well, I took health for granted. I am a strong, healthy person, can eat anything and sleep anywhere, can put in any amount of hours of work, can tough it out, can brave the sun in summer, the snow in winter, and the sickly wetness of the long monsoon months. I may have a passing headache or a sneezing cold, but I spurn medicines and ignore doctors, and I know that my trustworthy body can pull me through any crisis and defy any microbes or bacteria in the interest of my work, which cannot wait as it is work for people and for God. I am proud of my strength and count on it to keep on working without rest and living without care.

But now sickness has come, and I am down. Down in my body between the burning sheets of an infirmary bed and down in my soul under the humiliation and the perplexity of my broken strength. My head is reeling; my temples are throbbing; my whole body is aching; my chest has to force itself to breathe. I have no appetite, no sleep, no desire to see anybody, and above all no desire to be seen by anybody in my hour of misery, which looks as though it were to last forever. If my body fails me, how can I go on living any more?

My iniquities have overwhelmed me. They weigh like a burden too heavy for me. My wounds grow foul and fester because of my foolishness. I am utterly bowed down and prostrate: all day I go about mourning. My lungs are filled with burning pain, and there is no wholeness in my flesh.

But now, in the long hours of my enforced idleness, my thoughts turn, of necessity, to my body, and I begin to see it in a new light and to recover a relationship with it I should have never lost. My body's sickness is its language, its way of telling me that

I was misusing it, ignoring it, despising it, though it is very much part of me. As children cry when no attention is paid to them, so my body cries because I have neglected it. Those cries are its fever and its weakness and its pain. Now I listen to them and grasp their meaning and accept their wisdom.

My body is so close to me that I had taken it for granted, and now it tells me gently, painfully, reluctantly that it cannot put up with such neglect. Sickness is only a cleft between soul and body, between ideal and reality, between the impossible dream and the daily facts. Sickness brings me down to earth and reminds me of my human condition. I welcome now the reminder and hasten to reestablish a dialogue with my body, a dialogue that should have never been broken.

We'll go together through life, my dear body, hand in hand and heart to heart, with the rhythms of your flesh giving expression to the tides of thought and feeling that swell and ebb inside my mind. Smile when I rejoice, and tremble when I fear; relax when I rest, and tense every nerve when I concentrate on the problems of living. Warn me of coming dangers; signal your fatigue before it is too late, and radiate your approval when you feel fine and like my doings and enjoy life with me.

Thank you, Lord, for my body, my faithful companion and trusty guide in the paths of life. And thanks even for this sickness that brings me closer to it and teaches me to take care of it with love and providence. Thank you for reminding me of my whole self, of reuniting me again, of making me whole. And, as a sign of your blessing, as a recognition that this sickness came from you to awaken me to the totality of my being, heal now my body, which you have created, and restore to me the joy of health and strength to go on living with zest and confidence, to go on working for you, mindful now that it is not only my mind and my soul that work but my body with them in loving unity and faithful cooperation. When I pray, it is now the whole of me that prays to you.

Do not forsake me; O my God, be not far from me! Make haste to help me, my salvation!

Psalm 39

Prayer of the Tired

I am tired, Lord. I am fed up with life. People say that life is short. To me it now looks long, eternally long. I don't know what to do with my life. I could still live double the years I've lived, maybe three times more, and I shudder at the thought of it, the thought of the burden, the routine, the boredom of it all. It is not so much the suffering I complain of now, but the sheer weariness of living. To walk the same streets again, to do the same chores again, to meet the same people, to say the same meaningless words. Is that life? And if that is life, is it worth living at all?

"Yahweh, you have shown me my end." Let me know my end.

It seems a dreadful prayer, and yet it is my only consolation now. Let me know my end. Let me know that this dreary existence will come to an end, that one day it will be over and there will be no more walking without aim, no more living without meaning. Let me at least know that this will not go on forever, not for long, please; life is so painfully dull, so mercilessly repetitive.

I dread the chair on which I sit; I hate the table on which I write; I cannot bear the sight of these four walls that encompass my life and limit my existence. They speak of prisoners in jail. What does if matter if the jail has high walls or low, so long as I don't get out of them and so long as they determine my daily routine with deadly efficiency! Tomorrow's ways are the same as today's just as today's were the same as yesterday's and so on as far as my memory goes. "Making a living," that is what they call it. Has anybody yet thought of living a living?

I am tired, Lord, and you know it. Still I feel some relief in saying it before you, not as a complaint, not even as a prayer, if you understand me, but just as a confidence, a talk between friends, a letting off steam before one who understands and wants to listen in sympathy. Mine is the wayfarer's fatigue, and I want to sit on a stone by the wayside and forget for a moment the weariness of walking on the dusty road. I'll keep on walking, Lord, but let me rest for a while before starting again on the dull journey. The fact that you are near will give me the strength I need to continue.

Yahweh, hear my prayer. Listen to my weeping. I am a wanderer before you, a pilgrim like my ancestors: turn your gaze from me so that I may take a breath, before I leave, and cease to be!

Psalm 40

Open My Ears!

Open my ears, Lord, that I may hear your word, obey your will, and follow your law. Make me attentive to your voice, attuned to your accent, that I may at once recognize the messages of your love in the middle of the jungle of noise that surrounds my life.

Open my ears to your word, your Scriptures, your revelation in human sound to humankind and to me. Make me love the reading of the pages of Scripture, rejoice in their sound, and enjoy their repetition. Let them be music to my ears, rest to my mind, and comfort to my heart. Let them awaken in me an instant echo of recognition, of familiarity, of friendship. Let me discover a new meaning in them every time I read them, because your voice is fresh and your message comes straight from you today. Let your word be revelation to me, and be strength and joy in my journey through life. Give me ears to listen, to grasp, to understand. Make me sensitive to your word in your Scriptures, Lord.

Open my ears to your word in nature, too, Lord. Your word in the skies and the clouds, in the wind and the rain, in the icy mountains and in the fiery depths of this earth you have created for me to live on. Open my ears to your voice of power and of tenderness, your smile in a flower and your wrath in the tempest, your caress in the breeze and your warning in the peal of thunder. You speak through your works, Lord, and I want the ears and the faith to understand their meaning and live their message. Your whole creation speaks, and I want to be an eager listener to the intimate waves of your cosmic language—the grammar of the galaxies, the syntax of the stars. Your word that steadied the universe is to steady my heart now in blessing and in grace. Fill my ears with the sounds of creation and of your presence in it, Lord.

Open my ears also to your word in my heart. The secret message, the intimate touch, the presence without words. Divine telex of personal news. Let it sound; let it print; let it bring to me moment by moment the living remembrance of your permanent love. Let me hear your silence in my soul; let me guess when you smile and when you frown; let me sense your moods and respond to them with the ready sensitivity of deep faith and steady trust. Let us keep up the dialogue, Lord, without any break, without any blackouts, without any doubts, mistrust, or misunderstanding. Bring your loving word to my willing heart.

Open my ears particularly, Lord, to your word in my brothers and sisters. You speak to me through them, through their presence, through their needs, through their suffering, and through their joys. Let me hear the human concert of my race around me, the notes I like and the notes I dislike, the contrasting melodies, the valiant chords, the measured counterpoint. Let me hear every accent and pay attention to every voice. It is your voice, too, Lord. I want to be attuned to the global harmony of history and society, to join in it and let my life sound as part of it in meaningful accord.

Open my ears, Lord. Grace of graces in a word of sound.

Psalm 41

Concern for the Poor

Happy those who aid the poor and the lowly. God will help them when they are in trouble. Yahweh will protect and preserve them, will make them happy in the land.

Thank you, Lord, for your gift to your Church in our days: the gift of concern for the poor, of awareness of injustice and oppression, of awakening to liberation in the human soul and in the structures of society. Thank you for having shaken us out of our complacency with existing orders, out of acquiescence in inequality and temporizing with exploitation. Thank you for the new light and the new courage that have surged through your Church today to denounce poverty and to right oppression. Thank you for the Church of the poor.

You have moved our thinkers to think and our people of action to act. In our days theology has become liberation theology, and pastors of souls have become martyrs. You have opened our eyes to see in the poor our suffering brothers and sisters, members in pain, together with us, of the one body of which you are the Head. You have ended the days in which we wrongly understood conformity with your will as acceptance of injustice and exhorted the poor to remain poor as though that were your will for them. You don't want injustice, Lord, you don't want oppression, and we ask your pardon if we ever used the interpretation of your will to justify an unjust order. You have spoken again through your prophets, and we respond in gratitude to the call and the challenge you have put before us. We want to liberate your people again.

You always listened to the plea of the orphan and the widow and considered any injustice done to them as done to you. Now, Lord, it is whole peoples that are orphaned and entire sections of society that feel destitute as a widow without support and without help. Their cry has reached you, and you, in return, have raised a new conscience in us in order to make us feel solidarity with all those who suffer and in order to get to work to redress the wrongs that are inflicted on them. We feel privileged that our age has been chosen to be the age of liberation and our Church to be the Church of the poor. We accept with joy the responsibility of working for a new order in your name and of bringing justice among your children upon earth so that as all are equal in the love you bestow on them, so they may be equal in the use of the goods you have freely made available to all your children.

We make this pursuit the goal of our efforts and the aim of our life. We are glad to see a universal revival and want to contribute to it with our enthusiasm and our work. We feel strongly in our hearts a concern for the poor and count ourselves fortunate to have been given that grace by you. Thank you for that blessing on our generation.

Let us praise Yahweh, praise the God of Israel now and forever! Amen! Amen!

Book II

Psalm 42

Longing for the Lord

Like the deer that yearns for running streams, so my soul is yearning for you, my God. My soul is thirsting for God, the living God. When can I enter to see the face of God?

I long. I thirst. I yearn. Deep in my heart that yearning is the vital thrust of my life, the motive force of my earthly existence. I live because I long for you, Lord; and in a way, because I long for you, I die, too. Sweetest torture of loving at a distance, of seeing through a veil, of possessing in faith, and of waiting in impatience. I desire your presence as I desire nothing else in this world. I imagine your face; I hear your voice; I worship your divinity. I rest in the thought that if waiting for you is so sweet, what will it be meeting you!

I want to meet you in prayer, in your unmistakable touch during the moments in which my soul forgets everything around and is only in silence with you. You have a way of making yourself indubitably present to the soul that thinks of you in solitude. I prize those instances and treasure those visitations that anticipate heaven upon earth.

I want to meet you in your sacraments, in the reality of your pardon and in the hidden glory of your table with humankind. I come to you in faith; and you reward that faith with the fleeting whisper of the wings of your love. I will come again and again with the memory of those blessed encounters, the patience of waiting in darkness and the eagerness to feel your closeness anew.

I want to meet you in the faces of humankind, in the sudden revelation that all people are my brothers and sisters, in the need of the poor and in the love of my friends, in the smile of a child and in the noise of a crowd. You are in all people, Lord, and I want to recognize you in them.

And I want to meet you one day in the poverty of my being and the nakedness of my soul, in the face of death and the gateway of eternity. I want to meet you face to face in the moment that will be bliss forever, in the embrace of recognition after the night of life in this world.

I long to meet you, Lord, and the vehemence of that longing upholds my life and steadies my step. In that hope life has a meaning, and my earthly pilgrimage has a direction. I am coming to you, Lord.

Like the deer that yearns for running streams, so my soul is yearning for you, my God. My soul is thirsting for God, the living God. When can I enter to see the face of God?

Psalm 43

The God of My Joy

Give me the gift of joy, Lord. I need it for myself and for my brothers and sisters. This is no selfish prayer for my own contentment but a deep, social, and religious need to communicate to others your presence through the sacrament of your joy in the sincerity of my heart.

This world is a sad place for many, with their worries and their misery, their drudgery and their routine. Hardly a genuine smile, hardly a spontaneous laugh. There is a pall of gloom over the lives of humankind. It is only your presence, Lord, that can dispel that gloom and make the brightness of your joy shine, like the bursting of dawn, over the dreariness of life.

To communicate your joy to humankind, Lord, you want other people as channels and witnesses of the only true joy, which is your grace and your love. That is why I offer you my heart and my life, Lord, in order for you to touch other people by touching me. Make me rejoice with you, so that when I walk into another person's life I may illumine his or her face in your name and so that when I enter the company of other people I may brighten the place with your splendor.

Make my smile be sincere, and my laughter be genuine. Make my face shine with the reflection of your presence. Make my heart expand with the warmth of your grace. Let my step quicken and my body respond to the majesty of your glory. Bless me with joy so that I may bless, in turn, the persons I meet and the places I visit. Anoint me with happiness, that I may consecrate the world of humanity in the liturgy of rejoicing.

Men and women in this world want happiness, Lord, and if they see happiness in the people who follow you and profess your service, they will come to you to get for themselves what they have seen in your servants. If you want to save religion on earth, Lord, give joy to religious men and women. Your joy is our strength.

When I ask for joy, I do not shun trials and sufferings. I know the human lot on earth and accept it with willing faith. But in the midst of those trials and sufferings that form part of the human condition, I ask for the serenity to face them and the steadfastness to go through them with confidence, so that even in my dark hours I may be a living witness to the power of your hand. When I cannot have the glowing brightness of outward joy, let me have at least the soothing clarity of resigned acceptance. In peace and in joy let me always be a serene witness to the glory to come, a citizen of heaven, on my way through earth, to my final destination.

God of my delight and joy. That is my boast; those are my credentials; that is my confidence. Your joy is my light, my guide, and my strength.

Send forth your light and your truth—they shall guide me; let them bring me to your holy mountain, to your dwelling place. Then I will go in to the altar of God, the God of my delight and joy.

Psalm 44

Prayer for a Troubled Church

It is not that people attack us now, Lord, it is that they simply ignore us. The Church does not count any more in the minds of many. Its doctrine and its teaching, its rulings and its warnings are just set aside and politely passed over by most people. They don't take even the trouble to oppose us, to answer our arguments, or to consider our reflections. They just take no notice and go their way as though we did not exist, as though your Church meant nothing to the modern world. They tell us we are not relevant, and that is the worst charge that can be made against us in today's society. These are troubled times for your People, Lord.

We have been taken a little by surprise, because we were used to consideration and respect. The word of your Church was heard and obeyed; it ruled consciences and drew frontiers among peoples. Those were days of power and influence, and their memory is still with us.

O God, we have heard with our ears, our ancestors have told us all the deeds that you did in their days, all the work of your hands in days long ago. You planted them in the land and drove the nations out; you made them strike root, scattering the other peoples. It was not our ancestors' swords that won them the land, nor their arm that gave them the victory—but your right hand and your arm and the light of your face. Such was your favor to them.

We don't want to revert to an easy triumphalism by any means, but we feel we have been thrown from one extreme to the other. Formerly we were the center of the world, and now suddenly we don't seem to exist. In the military terms of your psalm, *But now you have rejected and humbled us and no longer lead our armies into battle.*

That is the sorrow of my heart: You don't lead us now into battle. I don't mean the battle of chariots and horses, the war of bombs and missiles; I mean the battles of the spirit, the conquests of the mind, the upholding of human values, and the victory of freedom over oppression. You don't fight on our side. We don't feel the power of your right arm. We speak and nobody listens, we plead and nobody takes notice. Human dignity is insulted, and human rights are trampled upon. And you don't seem to care.

You have exposed us to the taunts of our neighbors, to the scorn and contempt of all around. You have made us a byword among the nations, a laughingstock to the people, so my disgrace confronts me all day long, and I am covered with shame at the shouts of those who reproach and abuse me as the enemy takes revenge.

We don't ask for external glory but for inner conversion. We don't want public attention but spiritual efficiency. We don't want honor for us but love for all people. And you can do that as you did in former days.

Rouse yourself—why do you sleep? Awake, do not reject us forever. Why do you hide your face, forgetting our misery and our sufferings? For we sink down to the dust and cling to the ground. Rise up and come to our help; because of your unfailing love, set us free.

Psalm 45

A Song of Love

This is the song of a king and a queen, the wedding of a prince and a princess, the covenant between God and his People, the union between Christ and his Church. This is a poem of love between you and me, Lord: this is our private romance, our spiritual love feast, our mystical intimacy. No wonder *My heart overflows with a goodly theme . . . my tongue is like the pen of a ready scribe.*

How beautiful you are, prince of my dreams! *You are the fairest of all; grace is poured upon your lips; thus God has blessed you forever. . . . You love justice and hate wickedness, therefore God, your God, has anointed you with the oil of gladness; your robes are fragrant with myrrh and aloes and cassia. From ivory palaces, stringed instruments bring you joy. . . . Hear, O daughter, consider, and turn your ear; forget your people and your ancestor's home. The king will desire your beauty. The princess is decked in her chamber with gold-woven robes; in many-colored robes she enters with her virgin companions, her escort in her train.*

The heart of religion is love. Studies and discussions and scholarship and research are wonderful, but they leave me cold, Lord. I like to know about you, but there are times when learning about you becomes pure learning, and I forget you. Today I want to put everything aside and tell you simply and directly how wonderful you are, how much you fill my life and how much I love you—more than I love anything or anybody on earth. You are lovable beyond description, Lord, and your beauty holds me fast with the infinite charm you alone possess.

I have loved you from my childhood; I discovered your friendship in my youth; I fell in love with your Gospels, and I dreamt every day of the moment of meeting you in the Eucharist.

If there was ever romance in a young person's life, that was it! For me, faith is falling in love, religious vocation is looking at your face, and heaven is you. That is my theology, and that is my dogma. Your person, your voice, your smile. Prayer is being with you, and contemplation is looking at you. Religion is experience. "Come and see" is the summary of the four Gospels and the whole of Scripture. To see you is to love you, Lord, and to love you is bliss forever in this life and in the next.

As I have grown, my love has matured. It does not have now the impetuousness of the first meeting, but it has gained the depths of wisdom and age. I have learned to be silent with you, to trust, to wait, to know that you are there in the length of my days and the darkness of my nights. I am content to hold your hand in faith to seal the mutual trust that years of living together has built between us. I know you better, and I love you more as I spend my life with you in faithful company.

You have spoken of a wedding, of espousals, of bride and bridegroom, of prince and princess; you yourself have chosen a terminology I would not have dared to use, and I thank you for that and treasure the terms of our love in the boldness of your expressions. You have chosen the best words of human language, the most telling, the most intimate, to describe our relationship, and I now use those words with deep reverence and intimate joy. A lover knows how to select words, to nurse them, to fill them with meaning and to pronounce them with tenderness. I receive those words from you, Lord, lovingly, and return them to you with my own devotion and love. Prince of my dreams, may you be blessed forever and ever!

I will cause your name to be celebrated in all generations; therefore the peoples will praise you forever and ever.

Psalm 46

Be Still

"Be still! and know that I am God."

How much I need that admonition, Lord! On hearing it from you I feel that all my spiritual welfare, my progress, and my happiness are in it. If only I could learn to keep quiet, to relax, to let be in faith and confidence, I would find out that you are Lord and God, that the world is in your hands and I with it, and that in that realization I shall find joy and peace.

But that is, I confess, the one thing I don't know: how to keep quiet. I must move around and busy myself and hurry and worry. I keep doing things and planning reforms and urging improvements and driving myself and everybody mad with all sorts of activities. Even in my prayer life I plan and control and examine and improve continually what I do with the urge to do tomorrow better than today and to ensure that I keep moving forward in my worthy endeavor. I am a compulsive perfectionist, and I want to make sure that whatever I do, whether in my profession or in my prayer, has to be, without fail, the best I can do. That behavior upsets the balance of my mind and ruins my chances of finding you in peace.

I want to run my own life, not to mention the future of society and the destinies of humankind. I want to be in control, to order, to rule. And so I am always on the move, both in the multiplicity of my thoughts and in the urgency of my activities. That very hurry blinds me to your presence and makes me miss the offer of your power and your grace. I don't see you because I am too busy looking at myself. I fill my day with feverish activity, and I have no time for you. Then I feel empty without you and pack even more activity into my day to cover up its emptiness.

Futile endeavor! My dissatisfaction grows, and my distance from you increases. My life is in the deadly grip of that vicious circle.

And then I hear your voice: *"Be still! and know that I am God."* You bid me to calm down, to reduce speed, to enter silence. You want me to ease my own grip on life, to take things gently, to invite quietness. You ask me to sit down and look at you, to see that life is in your hands, that you direct the course of creation, that you are Lord and God. It is only in the peace of my soul that I can recognize your glory and majesty. It is only in silence that I can worship.

I know the meaning of those words when you first addressed them to Israel: *Come! See the deeds of the Most High, the marvelous things God has done on earth; all over the world, God has stopped wars.* Put down your weapons, stop your wars, quit defending your interests and obtaining your victories. Leave it to me, and then you will see how I am God and protect you and defend you. I have fought a lot for our cause, Lord. Teach me to stop fighting.

Your extended arm calmed the storms on the sea, Lord. Extend now your mighty hand over my heart to calm the storms that brood in it as in the blackness of a winter sky. Soothe my emotions; heal my anxiety; allay my fears. Make the blessing of peace descend at your bidding over my troubled heart. Pronounce again the word of counsel and power over me: *Be still*. And then, in the silence of wonder and the stillness of faith, I shall know that you are God, the God of my life.

Psalm 47

You Chose Our Land for Us

You divided the Promised Land among the tribes of Israel, Lord, and you have chosen for me the circumstances of history and family and society in which I am to live—my promised land, my inheritance, my "vineyard," in biblical terms. Today I want to thank you for my vineyard, to accept it from your hands, to tell you explicitly and openly that I like your choice of life for me, that I am proud of my age, at home in my culture, and happy in my land. It is a wonderful time to be alive, Lord.

I hear people compare and complain and regret and wish they had lived in another age and in other lands. That, to me, is heresy and rebellion. All times are good and all lands are blessed, and the time and the place you chose for me are doubly blessed in my sight because they were your personal choice, your caring providence, your loving gift to me. I like my vineyard, Lord, and I would not change it for any other, ever.

I love my body and my mind, my intelligence and my memory as you have given them to me. My vineyard. Many around me have healthier bodies and keener intellects, and I praise you for that, Lord, as you show glimpses of your beauty and your power in the living works of your creation. There are better vines and more luscious grapes in vineyards around mine. Still I value and treasure mine above all others, because that is your gift to me. You have chosen my inheritance for me, and I rejoice in it.

You choose for me the events that meet me during the day, the news I read and I hear, the weather that greets me, and the moods that assail me. You choose my land for me. Teach me now how to till that land, how to handle those moods, how to meet those people, how to profit by those events. I am a child of my time, and I see that time as given by you, so I want to work in it with faith and with joy, never with despondency or despair. This world is lovely because you have created it for me. Thank you for this world, for this life, for this land. Thank you for my vineyard, Lord.

Psalm 48

The City of God

Zion for me means Jerusalem, the earthly and the heavenly, the home of the People of God, the Church, the Promised Land, the City of God. I rejoice when I hear its name. I like to pronounce it, to sing it, to fill it with my dreams of that heavenly homeland, with the landscapes of my imagination, and with the colors of my longing. All that is good and beautiful is projected into the skyline of that ultimate city on the eternal hills.

Great is Yahweh and worthy of praise in the city of our God, whose holy mountain, fairest of heights, is the joy of all the earth. Mount Zion, far up in the north, is the city of the Most High.

A city has foundations and monuments and gardens and avenues, and the city of my dreams has all that in the perfection of its design and the glory of its architecture. It is a symbol of order and planning, of human beings living together and of nature's resources being harnessed for the welfare of its children. The city fits in the landscape, is part of it, is almost the horizon made geometry, the trees and the clouds blending in graceful harmony with the buildings and the towers of humankind's habitation. The perfect city in an ideal world.

I cherish my dream of my fair City, and then I open my eyes and prepare my day and get ready to walk the streets of the very real, human, earthly city I live in. I see crooked alleys and dirty corners; I pass by gloomy buildings and reeking huts; I see traffic and squalor; I smell the unventilated presence of humanity; I hear the cries of beggars and the wailing of children; I suffer in the midst of this living mockery of the City, the "polis," the "urbs," which has transformed the dream into a nightmare and the model of design into a blueprint of misery. I weep in the streets and squares of my tortured metropolis of today.

And then I open my eyes again, the eyes of faith, the eyes of wisdom and of knowledge, and I see my city, and, in it as figure and sign, I see the City of my dreams. There is only one city, and its appearance depends on the eyes that view it. This city of mine with its twisted alleys and its pungent smells was also created by God, that is, created by human beings who were created by God, which comes to the same thing. God also dwells in this city, in the dignity of its temples and in the lives of its inhabitants. This city is also sacred with the smoke of sacrifices and the shouts of jubilation. This is also the City of God because it is the city of human beings, and human beings are the children of God.

I rejoice now while I go through its streets, I mingle with its crowds, and I am caught in its traffic jams. I sing hymns of praise and glory at the top of my voice. Yes, this is the City and the Temple and the Tent of the Presence and the abode of the great King. My earthly city shines with the splendor of the human beings who dwell in it, and as humankind is the image of God so his city is the image of the heavenly City. I am glad at my discovery, which opens my heart and redeems my sojourn on earth. Blessed be your city and my city, O Lord.

Walk about Zion, go all around it. Count the towers. Study the ramparts well; examine the castles, that you may tell the next generation that such is God. Forever and ever our God will guide us.

Psalm 49

The Eternal Riddle

Hear this! Listen, all people everywhere, both great and small alike, rich and poor together. My heart is full of insight; I will speak words of wisdom. I will turn my attention to a proverb and unravel its meaning as I play the harp.

The riddle is the eternal riddle of all ages and all people. Why do the just suffer while the wicked prosper? Is it to test our faith, to try our patience, to enhance our merit? Is it to hide from our eyes the ways of God, to shake our complacency, to challenge our human calculations? Is it to tell us that God is God and will not be held to account by any human mind? Is it to remind us of the smallness of our minds and the meanness of our hearts?

Why do the just suffer and the wicked prosper? All philosophies have wrestled with the question; all wise men and all privileged minds have tackled the problem. Volumes upon volumes and discussion against discussion. Is God unfair? Is humankind stupid? Is life without a meaning?

People have approached the problem with their minds. The psalmist sings it with the harp. And there is wisdom and depth in the gesture of the psalmist. The depths of the mysteries of human life on earth are not to be thought but to be sung: they cannot be expressed through equations but through mysticism, they are not to be analyzed but to be lived.

Yes, there are things I don't grasp in life, many situations that pass my understanding, many problems beyond my ken. I can rack my brains trying to give an answer to questions that generations of the wise have not been able to answer, or I can simply, in realism and humility, take life as it comes and answer its questions by living them with sensitivity and commitment, with personal responsibility and social sense, with honesty in my actions and concern in my service. I prefer to handle riddles with my harp rather than with the point of the sword. I prefer to live my life than to spend it reasoning out how I ought to live it. I prefer to sing than to argue.

I accept the riddle of life, Lord, I trust your understanding of it when my own fails, and I commit myself and all people into your hands with trust and with joy. That is my practical way of showing that you are Lord of all.

Psalm 50

The Blood of Goats

This is my danger, Lord, in my prayer life, in my dealings with you: routine, repetition, formalism. I recite the prayers; I follow the rituals; I fulfill the requirements. But sometimes my heart is not in my prayers, and I say them out of habit; I go because everybody goes and I am supposed to go. I even feel some scruple and fear that if I omit my prayers you will be displeased with me and might even punish me, and so I go when I have to go, and I say what I have to say and sing what I have to sing but in a rather empty way, without devotion and without love.

What is worse, Lord, sometimes I am very careful with the rituals of the liturgy precisely because I have been negligent in the observance of your precepts. I pay attention to your service to make up for not having paid attention to my kin. And I fear you don't look kindly on that type of service.

Do I eat the flesh of strong bulls or drink the blood of goats?

You don't need my sacrifices, my offerings, my money, or my blood. What you want is the sincerity of my devotion and the love of my heart, and the manifestation of this love in my love to all people for your sake. That is the sacrifice you desire, and without it no other sacrifice will be pleasing to you.

Your words are harsh, but they are true when you rebuke me, Lord:

"What right have you to recite my laws or take my covenant on your lips? For you hate discipline, and you cast my words behind you. When you see a thief, you become friends; and you keep company with adulterers. You give your mouth free rein for evil, and your tongue frames deceit. You sit and speak against others; you slander your own family. These things you have done and I have been silent."

Yes, Lord, I admit it. I have often been unfair and unkind to my brothers and sisters, and what value can my sacrifices have when I have wronged my kin before approaching your altar? Thank you for reminding me, Lord, and opening my eyes to the true sacrifice you desire from me. No bulls and goats, no blood or ritualism, but love and service, kindness and righteousness, justice and availability. I must serve you through my kin before I can worship you at your altar.

And once I serve my kin in your name I want to ask of you the blessing that when I come to you in prayer I may also find you, I may see meaning in what I say and may put feeling in what I sing. Free me, Lord, from the curse of routine, of formalism, of taking you for granted, of converting religious practices into meaningless rubrics. Let every prayer of mine be a psalm, and, like a psalm, let me have joy in it and confidence and love. Let me be true to myself and true to my brothers and sisters, that I may be true to you.

"To those who order their way aright—I will show the salvation of God!"

Psalm 51

My Sin and Your Mercy

I have sinned against you and no other. That is my sorrow and my shame, Lord. I know how to be kind to others, I am a considerate person and like to be known and appreciated as such. I am polite and thoughtful and pride myself on keeping good relations with all and being faithful to my friends. I never hurt anyone or put anybody to inconvenience; it is not my way to do harm to people or to give them pain. And yet to you, you alone, I have given pain. I have betrayed our friendship and hurt your feelings. *I have sinned against you and no other.*

If you ask any of my friends or any of the people who live with me or work under me whether they have anything against me, they'll all say no. They'll say that I'm a nice person and, yes, I have my weak points (who hasn't?) but I am pleasant to live with and never say a harsh word or play a mean trick or let anybody down. They'll say that I am a dependable person and can be relied upon to stand by my friends if the need arises. Nobody has a complaint against me. Only you have. I have broken your law; I have ignored your wishes; I have disappointed you. In more serious matters I have trampled upon your blood and disowned your death. I, who never do that to anybody, have hurt you and let you down. *I have sinned against you and no other.* It was lust or it was pride; it was jealousy or it was spite; it was greed or it was selfishness. In any case it was me before you and me against you, because it was me against your law and your will and your creation. I have been ungrateful and rebellious; I have spurned a Father's love and a Creator's orders. I have no defense before you.

I have sinned against you and no other—knowing that my actions were wrong in your eyes. Your judgment is what I deserve; your sentence supremely fair. You can in all justice condemn me, Lord. I cannot refute your charge or reject your sentence. *My faults are always before me; my sins haunt my mind. . . . As you know I was born in guilt, from conception a sinner at heart.* I confess my sin, and, deeper down, I accept the fact that I am a sinner. That is my birth, my status, my definition. I, the whole of me—my mind and heart and soul and body as they are today at this moment before you, make me a sinner in your eyes and in my own conscience. I know it well when I do the evil I don't want and when I miss the good I wish I could do. I am conceived in sin, and I bear the weight of my sinfulness through the uphill path of my existence.

But though I am a sinner, you are a Father. You forgive and forget and accept. To you I come with faith and confidence, knowing that you never send your children away when they come to you with sorrow and humility.

In your goodness, O God, have mercy on me; with gentleness wipe away my faults. Cleanse me of guilt; free me from my sins. . . . Until I am clean, bathe me with hyssop; wash me until I am whiter than snow. Infuse me with joy and gladness; let these bones you have crushed dance for joy. Please do not stare at my sins; blot out all my guilt.

Let me feel clean again. Let me feel forgiven, accepted, and loved. If my sin was against you, my reconciliation must come from you. Give me your peace, your spirit, and your strength.

Create a pure heart in me, O my God; renew me with a steadfast spirit. Don't drive me away from your presence, or take your Holy Spirit from me. Once more be my savior; revive my joy. Strengthen and sharpen my still weak spirit.

Give me the joy of your pardon, that I may speak to others about you and your goodness and your mercy. *Open my lips, and my tongue will proclaim your glory.* Make my fall an occasion of my rising up, my drifting from you an opportunity to come closer to you. I know myself better now, as I know my weakness and my misery; and I know you better in the experience of your pardon and your love. I want to share with others the bitterness of my sin and the blessedness of your pardon. I want to proclaim before everybody the greatness of your merciful love. *And I will teach transgressors your ways; then sinners will return to you, too.*

Let the painful experience of my sin do good to myself and to others and to your whole Church, which is made up of people who want to come closer to each other and to you and who are hindered by the presence of sin upon the earth. Bless your People, O Lord.

Graciously show your favor to Zion; rebuild the walls of Jerusalem.

Psalm 52

The Razor and the Tongue

A modern metaphor in an ancient psalm: The slanderous tongue is razor sharp. It slashes; it cuts; it wounds. It brings forth calumny and insult and falsehood. Whenever it strikes, it hurts. It is a thing of danger and a tool of death, a deadly edge of spite, slander, and scorn. The human tongue can cause more harm than any weapon in hand.

The psalm defines the evil: *cruel gossip*. And I awaken with a shock to the burden of my daily irresponsibility. The gossip that so easily leaves my lips, that I utter in jest and carelessness, that I think to be just universal practice and forgivable fun, is in fact something hurtful, inhuman, cruel. I am cruel when I speak ill of others. I am merciless when I indulge in backbiting. I am heartless when I gossip. I destroy reputations; I damage relationships; I smear characters. And the smear remains because people are prone to believe the evil and ignore the good. There is destruction in my tongue, and I did not know it.

Your slanderous tongue is razor sharp. You love evil rather than good—falsehood, not speaking the truth. You love cruel gossip and slanderous talk.

Purify my speech, Lord. Curb my language and tame my words. Remind me, when I open my mouth, of the harm I can do, and direct all that I say to profit and to goodness and to help. I don't want to hurt anyone with the cutting edge of thoughtless words.

Psalm 53

The Death of God

I thought atheism was a relatively modern fashion. The talk on the death of God was almost news in the morning papers. Atheists and agnostics boast of being the latest thinkers against obsolete believers. And yet now I find in your psalms, Lord, that there were atheists already in those days. Already then people denied your existence and tried to convince themselves and others that there is no God. The disease seems to be an old one.

The fools say in their hearts, "There is no God."

I note the single word to describe the atheist and dismiss his case: fool. The biblical fool. The person that lacks wisdom, does not see far, does not perceive, does not understand. In this fool there is an absence of vision, of perspective, of sense, an incapacity to see what is before one's eyes, to take in the reality that emerges all around. These fools miss the point of life and do harm to themselves.

Am I not a fool at times also, Lord? Don't I behave as though you did not exist, blind to your presence and deaf to your warnings? I ignore you, I forget you, I bypass you. I live long hours and meet people and take decisions without ever a thought of you. I think and act at times as though you simply did not exist. I act on a purely human level, make my choices on human calculations and evaluate my results by sheer statistics. Am I not a practical atheist?

I want to fight atheism in the world today, and to do that I realize I have to begin by fighting it in my own life. I have to live and show a happy dependence on you in all that I do. I want to keep you before my mind when I think, to feel you in my heart while I love. I want to hear your voice and sense your presence, and I want to act always in such a way that your closeness to me appears and shines through my own actions. I want to be a believer not only in the recitation of my creed, but in the living out of each one of its words.

My answer to the "death of God" is that you, Lord, come truly alive in me.

Psalm 54

The Power of Your Name

Save me, O God, by the power of your name.

I worship your name, Lord, which my lips dare not pronounce. Your name is your power, your essence, your person. Your name is you. I rejoice at the thought that you have a name, you can be called, can be addressed, can enter into dialogue with humankind, can be dealt with as a person in confidence and familiarity. And I revere the silence of your anonymity in hiding your name from mortal knowledge and veiling your privacy with the mystery of your transcendence. Your name is above all names because your being is above all beings, the ground of all and the center of all.

Your name is written in the clouds and uttered in the sky among peals of thunder. It is etched in the profiles of mountain ranges against the snow and whispered in the murmurs of the waves in the ocean. Your name resounds in the name of everyone on earth and is blessed every time a child is baptized. All creation pronounces your name because all creation comes from you and goes back to you.

In the power of that name I trust. Whatever I am is also an echo of that sacred name. Don't permit that echo to die in barren silence.

Save me, O God, by the power of your name.

Psalm 55

Violence in the City

For I have seen violence and strife in the city. Day and night they go about on the walls; evil and trouble are in its center. Violence is within the city, and from the market place oppression and fraud are never absent.

That is my city, Lord, and that is happening in my time. Violence in the city. Strikes and agitations and police sirens and military raids. Streets that look like a battlefield and buildings that look like besieged fortresses. The clattering of automatic weapons and the report of bombs in the neighborhood. Houses on fire, markets deserted, and blood on the stones of the pavement. I have been in those buildings, and I have walked those streets.

I know the anguish of a twenty-four-hour curfew, the stinging bitterness of tear gas, the Dionysian frenzy of a crowd on wild rampage, the ominous news of violent death at a neighbor's doorsteps. The insecurity of the dark hours, the fear and the tension of enforced confinement at home, the uncertainty of the future, the weight of the black curse of vengeance on the hearts of humankind

This is my city, fair in its gardens and proud in its monuments. A city of long history and nourishing trade, of peaceful tradition and artistic design. A city built for people to dwell in in harmony, worship in its temples, learn in its schools, and meet in the open spaces of its urban embrace. A city I have loved through many years of living in the midst of it, watching it grow, and identifying with the many moods of its seasons, its feasts, its rains, its heat, its noises, and its smells. A city that is home to me, my address on earth, the resting place I come back to after every journey, with the warmth of my friends and the familiarity of its surroundings.

And now my city burns with fire and runs with blood. I feel shame and sorrow as I feel fear and disgust. I even feel the temptation to run away and find a safe refuge, free from the hatred and violence that here sadden and threaten my existence.

"Oh, had I the wings of a dove! Then I would fly away and be at rest. Yes, then I would flee far away and lodge in the desert. I would hasten to my place of refuge, from this raging wind and storm."

But I will not go away. I will stay in my city, bear its scars in my flesh and its shame in my soul. I will stay in the midst of violence, a victim to the passions of humankind in the solidarity of a common sorrow. I will fight violence by suffering its effects; I will win peace by enduring war. I will stay like the stones, the buildings, the trees of the city in loyal fidelity to it through adversity as through prosperity. I will redeem the sufferings of the city I love by taking them upon myself. Let those of good will walk together through tension and strife, that peace may return to the troubled city.

Cast your cares on God, who will sustain you and will never allow the righteous to fall.

Psalm 56

To Walk in Your Presence

To live is to walk. To keep going, to move ahead, to open new paths, to scan new horizons. Standing still is not living. That is passivity, inactivity, and death. Rushing is not living either. That is shooting through events without realizing what they are.

Walking keeps my feet in touch with the earth, my eyes open to the changing landscape, my lungs filled with new air at each step, my skin alert to the presence of the wind. At each moment I am fully where I am and fully moving to the next event in the gentle course that is my life. Walking is the most enjoyable sport in life, because living is the most enjoyable thing on earth.

And my walking is with you, Lord, by your side, in your presence. Walking in the presence of the Lord: that is what I want my life to be. The precious luxury of the leisurely step, the lost tradition of walking for its own sake, the silent companionship, the common direction, the ultimate end. Walking with you. Hand in hand. Step by step. Breath by breath. Knowing that you are there all the time, that you walk with me, and that you are enjoying my life with me. When I feel that you are enjoying my life with me, how can I not enjoy it myself?

For you have rescued me from death—to walk in your presence, in the light of life.

We'll keep walking, Lord.

Psalm 57

Your Purpose for Me

I call out to God the Most High, to God who has blessed me: to send from heaven and save me.

How consoling it is for me, Lord, to know that you have a purpose for me! I am not useless in your sight. I am not a routine creation, an accidental afterthought. A disposable production. I have been in your thoughts and in your plans from before the beginning of things. I was a thought in your mind before the stars shone and the planets in obedience found their orbits. I made sense to you before I ever made it to myself. There is a purpose for me in your heart, and that is enough for me to value my life and trust myself into existence. You see where I don't see, and you know what I don't know. You know me and count on me for your dreams of the Kingdom. You have a purpose for me. To discover it by living it out along my days is my very definition as a person. I want to be myself in faith till I find myself in you. That is my life.

You not only have a purpose for me, you fulfill it. In spite of my ignorance, my weakness, and my laziness, you carry out your plan and fulfill your purpose. You never force me, but gently lead me on with the mysteriously respectful and lovingly effective assistance of your grace. Your purpose will not fail, and your plan will not be frustrated. My own life rests now in the cosmic perspective of your infinite providence. The speck of dust has become a shining star. I am part of a glorious firmament, and I let its beauty and its majesty be reflected in the smallness of my being. Then the power of creation flows through me, and I am filled with the joy and the boldness to sing my song in the concert of creation. I have found my place in the world because I have found my place in your heart.

And this is my song: *My heart is steadfast, God, my heart is steadfast; I mean to sing and play for you. Awake, my soul awake, lyre and harp, I mean to wake the dawn! I mean to thank you among the peoples, to sing your praise among the nations. Your love reaches to the heavens, your faithfulness to the clouds. Rise high above the heavens, God, let your glory cover the earth!*

Psalm 58

The Curse of Deafness

Evildoers go astray all their lives; they tell lies from the day they are born. They are full of poison, like snakes; they stop up their ears, like a deaf cobra, which does not hear the voice of the snake charmer or the chant of the clever magician.

I think of myself and of the evil that is in me. I sometimes tell myself that I just don't hear your voice, so how can I proceed? Now I know that when I don't hear your voice it is because I have stopped my ears. The deaf cobra. The wily snake. It keeps its poison by closing itself to the charms of the flute in the hands of the skilled magician. Poison to kill others. Poison to make itself cursed among the creatures of earth.

I stop my ears and refuse to hear. I close myself in my stubbornness, and the poison of selfishness brews within me. Then, when I speak, I hurt; when I touch, I burn; when I move among others, I am feared and avoided. Those who know me sense the curse within me and keep away from me. I become the victim of my own poison, and I am left alone because I have proved myself dangerous.

Open my ears, Lord. Make me docile to your voice, open to your charms. Drain away the poison from inside me, that I may become and be recognized as harmless and friendly to all creatures and all people, that I may be admitted into their company and trusted in friendship.

Do not let me ever lose contact with you. Do not let me interrupt, be it only for a moment, my communication with you. Do not let me close my ears, turn my face, isolate my life. Even when I drift away from you, keep me always within hearing distance, call me, remind me. Do not give me up, Lord, and never allow me to ignore you.

The opposite of deafness is sensitivity, and that is the grace I ask of you above any other grace. To be open, alert, sensitive to you, to your presence, to your voice. Let me hear; let me listen. Let me always welcome your word to me, that my life may be the incarnation of your Word through me.

Psalm 59

My Tower of Strength

I turn to you, O God my Strength, for you are my stronghold.

On the horizontal landscape of the limitless plain there is a vertical shaft pointing to the heavens. Work of humankind between two works of God. Stone upon stone. Daring height over silent wastes. Safety from danger. Perpetual watch over unfriendly land. The watchtower. The timely warning. The trusty refuge.

I prize the symbol and make it mine. I need that tower. I need strength to face life, and I find none in me. I need firmness of thought, of will, of patient perseverance, and of living faith. I need courage to stand in the midst of a threatening world. I need steadfastness when everything around me shakes and wobbles and crumbles and falls. I need the comfort to know that there is a place where I can be safe, from which I can see far and watch the paths that lead to my heart. I need a tower in the topography of my surroundings.

You, Lord, are the tower of my life, my tower of strength. In you my doubts disappear, my fears vanish, my wavering ceases. I feel my own strength grow within me when you stand by me and lend me, by your very presence, confidence and faith. I thank you for putting that image into my mind, that reality into my life.

I will sing of your power . . . because you have been my stronghold, a shelter in the time of my trouble. My Strength, I always turn to you; for you, God, are my fortress, the God who loves me.

Psalm 60

The Fortified City

Who will bring me into the fortified city?

This has been my prayer for life, my daily longing, the aim of all my efforts and the crown of all my hopes. To enter the city. To penetrate its walls, to get past its fortresses, to reach its heart—yes, its heart—not only its heart of cobbled stones in the central square that rules its map and its life with the speed of its traffic and the efficiency of its business, but the heart of its culture: its history. The heart of its social life: its character, its personality. I want to enter the city. I want to reach its heart.

I live in the city, but, in a way, out of the city. Not quite part of it, not quite accepted, not quite belonging. Surely I pay taxes to the municipality and vote in its elections, I am a citizen in full right; I drink its water and board its buses. I can shop in its bazaars and relax in its gardens; I know the labyrinth of its streets and the design of its skyline. And yet I know I am not quite part of the city I call mine.

I feel a stranger in my city, or rather the city is a stranger to me. Alien, cold, remote. The city is secular. And I, because you are with me, am sacred. I bring your presence with me, Lord, whenever I walk into the city, and that makes my steps sound strange in the bustle of profane noise. I represent you, and you, Lord, have no place in the planned capitals of modern humanity.

The bulwarks and battlements of the modern city are against you, Lord, and against me in so far as I represent you. They are not masonry walls or crenelated towers; they are more subtle and more formidable. These bulwarks are materialism, secularism, and indifference. People have no time; people don't care. The things of the spirit find no place in the human city. There is no question of vanquishing armies but of winning attention; we don't want to obtain a victory; we just want to obtain a hearing. And that is the most difficult thing to obtain in this busy world of indifferent people.

I want to walk into the city, not with the anonymous curiosity of a tourist but with the message of a prophet and with the challenge of a believer. I want to make you present in the city, Lord, with the urgency of your love and the totality of your truth. I want to enter the city in your name and with your grace to sanctify in public consecration the human habitation.

Who will bring me into the fortified city? Only you can do it, Lord, as the city is yours by right. Your words proclaim your dominion over all cities in the land: *"In triumph I will apportion Shechem, and measure off the valley of Succoth. Mine is Gilead, and mine Manasseh; Ephraim is the helmet for my head; Judah, my scepter. Moab shall serve as my washbowl; upon Edom I will set my sandal. I will triumph over Philistia."*

The city is yours, Lord. *Who will lead me into Edom?* Who will take me into the heart of the city where I live, who will make me present where I already am, who will bring down prejudice and ignorance and indifference to open the way for the light not only in the privacy of the human heart but in the meetings and groups of open ways and public squares? Who will pull down the walls of the fortified city?

Edom is yours, Lord. Make it mine in your name, that I may consecrate it back to you.

Psalm 61

My Tent in the Desert

Life is a desert, and you, Lord, are my tent in it, always ready to shelter me from the rays of the sun and from the sands in the storm, ready help and constant safety. Without the promise of the tent I would never venture into the hostility of the desert.

You teach me through images, Lord. You have called yourself my rock, my fortress, my tower of strength, and now my tent. If the rock and the tower spoke of power and strength, the tent speaks now of companionship, of closeness, of being together in the intimacy of a reduced space through the thousand vicissitudes of a desert journey. Blessed be the desert that brings me closer to you in the shadows of your tent!

Lift me up and set me high upon a rock. For you have been my shelter, a tower of strength against the enemy. In your tent will I make my home forever and find my refuge under the shelter of your wings.

Psalm 62

Steadfast Love

You, Yahweh, are steadfast love.

There is no word we use more here on earth than the word "love." Love is the highest aspiration, the noblest thought, the deepest pleasure of humankind on earth. And yet there is no word more misused than "love." It is made to stand for base passions and fleeting feelings; it is stained with infidelity and marred by violence. Good people have to refrain from using the word to avoid its unhappy connotations.

Even when I come to religion and prayer and my relationship with you, Lord, I use the word "love." I am emboldened by your grace and your benevolence to say "I love you," and yet I realize how little I say when I say that, what an inconstant thing my love is, how unreliable, how superficial, how weak. I see the limitations and imperfections of my love, and I also feel inclined to abstain from using the word, I don't find true, steadfast love on earth, not even in my own heart.

That is why it now fills me with consolation to realize that somewhere at least I can find true, steadfast love, and that is in you, Lord. *You, Yahweh, are steadfast love.* In fact that is your very essence, your definition. You are love, you are the only true, steadfast love, pure, firm, eternal. I can now pronounce the word and recover its value. I can now believe in love because I believe in you. I can renew my hope and regain my courage to love, because I know there is one true, steadfast love, and that is close to me.

I now can love because I believe in your love. I know and I sense myself loved with the only true, steadfast love that exists: your own eternal love. That knowledge gives me the strength and the confidence to go out myself in love, to you first, and then in you and through you to all those you put close to me in my life. True, steadfast love is yours, Lord, and in faith and humility I make it now my own to love all in your name.

Psalm 63

Thirst

O God, you are my God whom I eagerly seek; for you my flesh longs and my soul thirsts like the earth, parched, lifeless, and without water. I have gazed toward you in the sanctuary to see your power and your glory.

That is the one word that defines the state of my soul, Lord: thirst. Bodily thirst, an almost animal thirst that burns my body and parches my throat. The thirst of the desert, of the dry sands and the scorching sun, of dunes and mirages, of desolate wastes and merciless skies. The thirst that overcomes every other desire and overrules any other need. The thirst that needs the draught of water to live, to subsist, to restore sensing to the body and rest to the soul. The thirst that mobilizes every cell and every sense and every thought to search for the nearest oasis and reach it before life itself is scorched to death in the body.

Such is my desire for you, Lord. Thirst in my body and in my soul. Thirst for your presence, your vision, your love. Thirst for you as you are. Thirst for the waters of life, which alone can bring peace to my desolate mind. Running waters in the midst of the desert, miracle of light and freshness, streams of delight, play of singing speed and dancing currents through dry earth and rocky ground. Presence in the night and melody in silence. I long for you. I trust in you. I rest in you.

Increase my thirst, Lord, that I may intensify my search for the fountain of life.

Psalm 64

Arrows

Flying arrows are messengers of death. Silent, pointed, deadly. The weapon most feared by the warriors of Israel. They cannot be seen. They cannot be parried. They strike from far, unknown and undetected, with death on their wings, and find with cruel accuracy the human target in the shadows of the night. Sword can be fought with sword, and dagger with dagger, but the arrow comes single and treacherous from an anonymous hand in the distant safety of enemy land. Its sharpened swiftness strikes helpless human flesh, and its needle point instantly reddens into gushing blood. Arrows are fateful death on winds of hatred.

The human word is an arrow. It flies and it kills. It carries poison, destruction, and death. A small word can ruin a life. A mere insult can build an enmity between two families for generations. Words can cause wars and plot murders. Words hit and wound humankind's noblest depths, honor, dignity, the peace of the human soul, and the value of the human name. Words threaten me in a world of blinding jealousy and ruthless competition. And then I pray.

Hide me from the conspiracy of the wicked, from the turbulent mob of evildoers who sharpen their tongues like swords and aim their cruel words like arrows. In ambush they shoot down the innocent, shooting suddenly, themselves unseen.

I ask for protection against the words of humankind, and the protection that is given me is the Word of God. Against the arrows of humankind, the arrow of God.

But God shoots them down with arrows. Their overthrow is sudden.

One arrow against all. God's Word against the words of humankind. God's word in Scripture, in prayer, in Incarnation and Eucharist. His presence, his strength, his Word. It illumines my mind and steadies my heart. It gives me courage to live in a jungle of words without fear of evil. God's Word gives me peace and joy forever.

The righteous rejoice and seek refuge in God, and all the upright praise God.

Psalm 65

The Rainy Season

It is raining today. With the oriental fury of a heathen monsoon. I watch the curtain of water, the instant Niagara, the running streets, the leaden skies, the violent descent of heaven upon the naked earth with waters of creation and waters of destruction on the liquid horizon where sky, land, and sea seem to be one with the primeval celebration of cosmic unity. The dance of the rain, of the children in the rain—rite of spring that seals the eternal covenant of humankind with nature and renews it year by year to bless the earth and multiply its crops. Liturgy of showers in the open temple where all humankind is one.

I rejoice in the rain; it makes the earth fertile, the fields green, and the air transparent. It brings out the perfume hidden in the dryness of the earth and fills with its humid delight the open spaces at the dawn of spring. It tames the heat, veils the sun, cools the air. It guarantees the fruits of the earth for the needs of the year and renews the farmer's faith that God will keep his word year by year and send the rains to give food to humankind and cattle as proof of his care and sign of his providence. The rain is God's blessing on the earth he created, renewed contact of the Divinity with the material world, seasonal reminder of his presence, his power, his concern. The rains come from above and enter deep into the earth below. God's touch on simple mud, which is the initial gesture of creation.

You have cared for the land and watered it; greatly you have enriched it. God's streams are filled; you have provided the grain. Thus have you prepared the land: drenching its furrows, breaking up its clods, softening it with showers, blessing its yield.

I also love the rain, the heavy, noisy, material rain, because it is figure and token of another rain that also comes down from heaven to earth, from God to human, from Divine Providence on the dry, barren fields of the human heart, unprepared for the harvest of the spirit. Rain of grace, showers of blessing, water of life. I feel the helplessness of my untilled fields, clods of dry earth between ridges of indifference. What good can come out of them? What crop can grow here? How can my field become soft and green and flower into harvest?

I need the rain of grace. I need the steady influx of God's power and mercy to soften my heart, to fill it with the fragrance of spring and make it fruitful. I depend on the grace of heaven as the farmer depends on its rains. And I trust in the coming of grace with the age-old trust the farmer has in the advent of the seasons and the faithfulness of nature.

I need torrential rains to wash away the prejudices, the bad habits, the conditionings, and the addictions that beset me. I need the freshness of the falling rain to feel again the reality of my wet skin through all the artificiality of protective covers under which my real self hides. I want to play in the rain like a child, to recover the pristine innocence of my heart under grace.

That is why I like heavy steady rain and make every drop into a prayer, every downpour into a reminder, every storm into an anticipation of what my soul expects to happen to it as happens to trees and flowers and fields. The green renewal of the season of rains.

Then my soul will sing for itself the psalm of the fields after the blessing of the yearly rains:

You have crowned the year with your bounty and with abundant harvest. The fallow meadows overflow, and gladness clothes the hills. The fields are arrayed with flocks, and the valleys blanketed with grain. They shout and sing for joy.

Come, blessed rain, and soak me to my heart!

Psalm 66

Come and See

Come and see what God has done.

Come and see. The invitation to experience. The chance to be present. The challenge to witness. *Come and see.* To me these three words are the essence of faith, the heart of mysticism, the core of religion. Come. Don't sit down quietly waiting for things to happen to you. Get up and start and move and search. Come close, enter. Face the reality you have been called to meet. And then see. Open your eyes, watch, see for yourself. Don't just listen or read or study. You have spent all your life in readings and studies and discussions and abstractions. All that is good, but is only second-hand evidence. It has to be transcended in faith and courageous humility in order to seek the firsthand evidence of vision and presence. *Come and see.* Seek and find. Enter and enjoy. The Lord has summoned you to his court.

I now take those hallowed words as said by you, Lord, to me. *Come and see.* You invite me to be by your side and to see your face. Your words are unmistakable, and your invitation is deliberate and serious. Yet I fight shy; I hold back; I find excuses. I am not worthy. I've been told it's safer to walk in the darkness of faith so I'll stick to the trodden path; I'll keep my place and hold my peace. I leave to my betters the mystic claims of your face-to-face vision and feel content with the life of routine that waits in patience for the plenitude to come. I am afraid, Lord. I don't want to get into deep waters. I feel comfortable where I am and beg to be left unmolested. The heights are not for me.

I am afraid that if I see you my life will have to change, my attachments will drop and my routine will be upset. I am afraid of your presence, and in that I feel one with the people of Israel, who delegated to Moses the responsibility of meeting you because they were afraid to do it themselves. It is my laziness, my inertia, my cowardice. Ultimately, it is my lack of trust in you, and, maybe, in myself. I acknowledge my pusillanimity and ask you not to withdraw your invitation from me.

I want to come and see your works, to come and see you at work, to contemplate you, to see the splendor of your face as you rule the vastness of your creation and the depths of the human soul. I want to see you, Lord, in the light of faith and the intimacy of prayer. I want the direct experience, the personal encounter, the effulgent vision. Devout people in all religions speak of the experience that changes their lives, the realization that fulfills their aspirations, the illumination that gives meaning to their existence. I humbly want that illumination for me, and it is your face alone that can shed that light on my mortal eyes. I want to see, and by that I mean that I want to see you who are the only reality worth seeing, you who, with the light of your face, give light to the whole of creation and to my own life. That is now my only desire and my ultimate hope.

Come and see.

I am coming, Lord. Give me the grace to see.

Psalm 67

The Missionary's Prayer

May God continue to bless us; and let God be feared to the very ends of the earth.

That is my prayer, Lord. Simple and direct in your presence and in the midst of the people I live with. Bless me, that all people round me may know you and love you in me. Make me happy, that, seeing me happy, all those who seek happiness may be attracted to me, and, in me, attracted to you who are the cause of my happiness. Show your power and your love in my life, that those who see my life may see you and praise you through me.

See, Lord: round me people each worship their own gods, and some worship none. They expect from their beliefs and from their rituals the divine blessings that will bring happiness to their lives as a token of the eternal happiness that will be granted them later. They measure, with human logic, the truth of their religion by the peace and joy it brings its followers, and they look at me to measure with expectant curiosity the peace and joy that I honestly and truthfully experience in my life and that I explicitly declare come only from you, Lord. They judge you by me, Lord, however awkward I feel when saying that, and so all I ask you is that you bless me in order that people around me may think better of you.

That was the situation of Israel. Each tribe around them had a different god, and each expected its god to bless them more than their neighbors' gods could bless, and in particular they expected their gods to give them better crops than their neighbors' gods could give. Israel prayed to you to give them the best crops in the region in order to show that you were the true God in heaven. And that is what I pray for now. Give me a visible crop of virtues and righteousness and happiness and joy, that all people around me may see your power and adore your majesty.

God, show your faithfulness, bless us, and make your face smile on us! For then the earth will acknowledge your ways, and all the nations will know of your power to save.

I want people to praise you, and so I ask you to bless me. If I were a hermit in a cave you could ignore me, but I am a Christian in a non-Christian society. I represent you; I take your place down here. Your name is in me; your reputation almost depends on me, Lord, so far as these people are concerned. That gives me a right to ask with urgency, if not with any merit, that you bless my life and direct my conduct in the face of all those who watch me and want to judge you by me and your sanctity by my behavior.

Bless me, Lord, bless your people, bless your Church; give us an unfailing crop of deep holiness and generous service that all may see our works and praise you for them. Make green the fields of your Church, Lord, for the glory of your name.

Let the nations praise you, God; let all the nations praise you! The soil has given its harvest; God, our God, has blessed us.

Psalm 68

From Sinai to Zion

I know that life is a journey, and I want mine to be a journey from Sinai to Zion with you as the Leader. Sinai was your voice, your command, your promise to lead your people into the Promised Land, and Zion is the stable city, the mighty fortress, the holy temple. My life, too, goes with your people, from mountain to temple, from promise to reality, from hope to glory through the long desert of my earthly existence. And with me all the days of my life goes your presence, your help, and your unfailing guidance through the sands of time. With you I feel safe in my journey.

O God, when you went forth before your people, when you marched through the wilderness, the earth quaked, the heavens poured down rain at your presence. Sinai quaked at your presence, O God.

The pilgrimage is hard at times. There are dangers and enemies, there is the weariness of the journey and the doubt whether it will ever come to an end, a happy end. There are strange names in the long geography, threatening kings at every turn of the map. The peaks of Bashan are jealous of the hill of Zion, and the enmity of neighbors plots harm against the transit of the Ark that carries your Presence. But it is that very Presence that gives protection and victory in the daily encounters of the faith pilgrimage.

Let God arise; let all God's enemies be scattered. . . . Sing to God, sing praises to God's name. . . . Father of the fatherless, mother of the orphan, and protector of the weak is God. God gives the forsaken a home in which to dwell and leads out the prisoners to freedom; but the rebellious dwell in a parched land.

The strength of my pilgrimage is to realize that it is also yours. You are the Lord of the desert, you are the Lord of life. With you you carry your people and me with them. I rejoice as the least member in the holy procession, the Benjamin in the tribes of Israel.

Your solemn processions are seen, O God, the processions of my God into the sanctuary—the singers in front, the minstrels behind, among them youth playing timbrels: "Bless God in your great congregation, O you who are of Israel's fountain!" There is Benjamin, the least of the tribes in the lead, the royalty of Judah in their throng, the royalty of Zebulun, the royalty of Naphtali.

To walk in the company of your people: that is my joy, Lord, and that is my protection. To feel one with your people, to fight in its battles, to grieve at defeat and to exult in victory. You are my God because I belong to your people. I am no lonely traveler, no solitary pilgrim. I form part of a people that marches together with one faith, one Leader, and one destiny. I know its history, and I sing its songs. I live its traditions, and I cling to its hopes. And as a closer and daily sign of my belonging to your people I renew and strengthen my union in friendship with the close group with which I live in your name. Cell of your Body and image of your Church. They are my companions given by you, and with them I walk and I strive, I relax and I play in the intimacy of a family, which mirrors in humble miniature the universality of the whole human family under you as a Father.

Rouse your power, O God; show your strength, as in the past. Because of your Temple at Jerusalem, rulers bear gifts to you.

In a way we have already arrived at the end of the journey. We are in Jerusalem, we are in your Temple, we are in your Church. *Let the righteous be joyful; let them exult before God; let them be jubilant with joy!* The joy of knowing that we are already in faith where we shall be forever in perfect fruition. The joy of a journey that is already crowned with the anticipation of the arrival. The joy of the traveler joined with the satisfaction of the inhabitant. We are pilgrims and citizens, we are on the way, and we have arrived, we claim both Sinai and Zion for our heritage. With you by our side we journey with joy and arrive in glory.

Blessed be God, our Savior, who bears our burdens day after day. Our God is a God of salvation.

Psalm 69

The Burden of Living

O God, rescue me! The waters are up to my chin.

I'm tired of life. I'm weary of the dismal business of living. I see no meaning in my life, no sense in going on when there is nothing to live for. I have cheated myself long enough with false hopes. Nothing comes true. Nothing makes sense. Nothing fits in. Oh, you know I've tried all my life; I've been patient; I've hoped against hope, and nothing has ever happened. There were glimpses at times, and I told myself that, yes, later on, some time, some day, light was sure to come and make everything clear and light up my way and show the final goal. But it never came. Finally I've been forced to be honest with myself and to admit the fact that all that was moonshine and make-believe and that I was in the dark as I've always been. I'm up against a wall, and the wall is dark granite that doesn't yield. I've reached the end of everything. I'm tired of life. Let me go, Lord.

I am wallowing in quicksand with no foothold for safety. I have slipped into deep water; the waves pound over me. I am exhausted from calling; my throat is parched. My eyes are strained with looking for my God.

My failure weighs on me, Lord, but even more than my failure it is your own failure, Lord, if you allow me to speak so, that bears me down and crushes me. Yes, Lord, your failure. Because if human life is a failure, it is you who made it, and yours is the responsibility for its breakdown. So long as only my sorrow was concerned I found refuge in the thought that my suffering did not matter provided your glory was safe. But now I see that your glory is intimately bound up with my happiness, and it is your name that suffers when my life goes black. How can you, my

Lord, keep your name unsullied when I, your servant, sink in the mud?

I have become an outcast to my ancestors, a foreigner to my family. Zeal for your house consumes me. The insults of blasphemers fall upon me.

For you and for me, then, Lord, save me and don't let my soul perish in despair. Bring me up; give me light; make life bearable for me, if not understandable. Save me for the glory of your name.

Rescue me from this swamp; let me sink no longer! Deliver me from my foes. Save me from the deep waters. Do not let the flood overwhelm me, nor the abyss swallow me up, nor the pit close its mouth over me.

All I ask for is a glimpse, a word, a window in the darkness that envelops me. A ray of hope in the night of despair. A reassurance that you are there and that the world is in your hand and that all will be well. Let the clouds part, if only for an instant, that I may see blue above and be reminded that the heavens exist and the way up is open for kind thoughts and fond hopes. Let me feel your power in the relief of my helplessness.

Protect me, O God, with your saving help. I will praise your name in song, and I will glorify you with thanksgiving.

O Lord, reconcile me again with my life!

Psalm 70

Do Not Delay!

I know the virtue of waiting, Lord, but I also know times in my life when waiting is not possible and the urgency of desire overrides every patience and clamors for your presence and your help. My endurance is limited, Lord, very limited. I respect your timetable and worship your divine will, but I burn with impatience, Lord, and it is useless for me to try to hide the imperativeness of my need under the cloak of my conformity. I know that you are here, that you can do, that you will act, and I cannot bear the delay of your action when I believe in the readiness of your love.

O God, make haste to rescue me. Come to my aid!

I have noticed how the days shorten when winter comes. As the winter of life approaches, my days also feel shorter and shorter, and I fear life will ebb away before I do what I want to do and reach where I want to reach, that is, before I reach you and achieve wholeness in your presence. The fear that freezes my bones is the fear that soon may be too late, that when I wake up I may have missed the chance, that my life may be wasted and my ideals may be left unrealized. Yes, I trust that in your mercy you will not reject me, but the fullness of my life, the dreams of my faith, the longing of my heart may still be left unfulfilled in this brief existence of mine. That is why I pray: Make haste, Lord; do not delay!

Have I not waited enough? Have you not counted my long years of training, my hours with you, my studies, my vigils, my unremitting efforts and my undefeated hopes? Is all that not enough? What more do I have to do to obtain your grace and change my life? Always the same miseries, the same shortcomings, the same temper, the same lust! I've put up with myself long enough. I want to change, to be a new person, to please you and to make life pleasant for those who live with me. I don't expect miracles, but I claim some improvement.

I want to feel your influence, your power, your grace, and your love. I want to be a witness in my life to the saving presence I acknowledge in you by faith. I want to do well, I want to be kind, I want to be faithful to you. With all my limitations, which I accept, I want to be loyal and true. For that I want your help, your blessing, your grace.

As for me, I am needy and poor; come to me, O God. You are my deliverer and my help. O God, do not delay.

Psalm 71

Youth and Old Age

Yahweh, I have trusted you since my youth; I have leaned on you since I was born. You have been my strength from my mother's womb and my constant hope. . . . Do not reject me now that I am old, nor forsake me now that my strength is failing.

You have been in my life, Lord, for as far as my memory goes back. That is my joy and my boast. My childhood, my youth, and my adulthood have all been under the shadow of your hand. I learned your name from my mother's lips, I called you friend before I had any other friend, I uncovered my soul to you as I did to no one else. I look back on my life, and I see it full of you, Lord, in my thoughts and in my joys and in my sorrows. I have walked with you through lights and shadows, and that is, in the smallness of my humility, the greatness of my call. Thank you for being with me through my life, Lord.

Now my years are beginning to get behind me, and I find myself thinking, almost against my will, of the years to come. Life is slowly climbing to its peak, and my eyes turn inevitably to the clouds that veil the end that looked so remote and now begins to appear close. Age begins to tell, to feel uncomfortable, to bring the uneasy thought that the time left for life may be already less than the time that has gone by. Hardly had I overcome the insecurity of youth when I find myself thinking of the insecurity of old age. My strength is not what it used to be, my memory is less reliable, my step is slower, and my senses are losing something of their sharpness. I soon will need the help of others, and that thought makes me sad.

More yet than the weakening of my senses I feel the ominous increase of the shadow of loneliness on my soul. Friends have died, ties have been loosened, attitudes have changed, and I find myself protesting against the new generation only to realize that by doing that I am placing myself with the old. There are fewer and fewer people around me with whom I can freely share my views and air my feelings. I've grown suspicious; I don't understand well; I don't even hear well, and I take refuge in a corner seat when all sit round the table, in silence when all talk. Loneliness is growing on me as the ghost of death on the stones of a cemetery. The sickness against which there is no remedy. The ebb of life. The burden of old age. The harbinger of death.

I feel fear when I think those thoughts, and I realize that from now on the way only narrows and will never broaden again. I feel fear of sickness, of inability, of solitude, of death. And I turn to you, Lord, who are my only help in my fears, my only support in my infirmity. You have been with me in my youth; be also with me in my old age. You have ruled over the first part of my life; rule over the last too. Sustain me when all others fail me. Relieve my solitude when all abandon me. Give me comfort; give me strength; give me the grace to age well, to feel kindly till the end, to smile till the last moment, to make younger people feel, by my example, that life is friendly and age a blessing, that there is nothing to fear and everything to hope for when God is by your side and your life is in his hands.

Lord of my youth, be also the Lord of my old age!

God, you taught me when I was a child, and I am still proclaiming your marvels. I am old, and now my hair is gray. O God, do not forsake me.

Psalm 72

Prayer for Justice

Israel's prayer for its king was a prayer for justice, for right judgment, and for the defense of the oppressed. My prayer for my country's government and for the governments of all countries is also a prayer for justice, equity, and liberation.

O God, with your judgment and with your justice, endow the leaders. They shall govern your people with justice and your afflicted ones with righteousness. The mountains will bring peace for the people, and the hills justice. They shall defend the afflicted among the people, save the children of the poor, and crush the oppressor.

I pray for just structures, for social awareness, for human concern between people, and therefore between group and group, class and class, and nation and nation. I pray that the stark reality of poverty today may come to view before the conscience of every person and every organization to shake every human heart and every ruling power into moral responsibility and efficient action to bring bread to every mouth, shelter to every family, and dignity to every person on earth.

When I pray for others, I wake myself and translate into my own situation what I wish for others in prayer. I am no monarch, and the destinies of nations do not hang on the words of my lips, nor can they be changed by the stroke of my pen. But I am a human being, a member of society, a cell in the body, and the currents of my feelings run through the nerves that sensitize the whole body into understanding and action. I pray that I may be so much alive with the need of reform that my thoughts and my words and the very look of my eyes and the spark of my step may kindle in others the same zeal and the same urgency to uproot inequality and establish justice. It is the task of all, and so for me it is my task, to be communicated in full conviction and enthusiasm to all those who in one way or another come into contact with me.

Israel will continue to pray for its king: *For they shall rescue the poor when they cry out and the afflicted when they have no one to help them. They shall have pity for the needy and the poor; they shall save the lives of the poor. From oppression and violence they shall redeem them, and precious shall their blood be.*

Then the Lord will bless the king and his people:

May they endure as long as the sun and like the moon through all generations. They shall be like rain coming down on the field, like showers watering the earth. Virtue shall flower in their days, and world peace till the moon is no more.

Book III

Psalm 73

The Pangs of Envy

When my heart had been growing sour and I was pained in my innermost parts, I had been foolish and misunderstood.

I am ashamed of myself, but I cannot help feeling envy. Why should I burn when others triumph? Why should I feel sad when others succeed? Why cannot I rejoice when others are praised? Why have I to force myself to smile when I congratulate them? I want to be kind to them, I recognize that their work is different from mine and their success does me no harm. On the contrary, they, in their own way, are also fostering the cause of your kingdom which is my aim too, so I should rejoice when they achieve something for your glory. But instead of seeing your glory in it, I see their glory, and I chafe at it. There is no more dismal sadness in the human heart than the sadness of grieving at the good of another.

And yet that sadness is in me. The seed of bitterness. The shame of jealousy. The pangs of envy. The most irrational suffering in the world, and yet the most real, actual, and daily. Hardly a day goes by, hardly an hour without the misery of senseless pride gnawing at my unhappy heart.

Then I seek justification for my insanity, and I cover with philosophical questioning the indefensibility of my complaints. Why do the good suffer? Why do the wicked prosper? Why do those who hardly ever address you get ahead of me who address you daily? Why do you suffer the irreligious to do well while deeply religious people are left in misery? Why is the world upside down? Why is there no justice on earth? Why is it you don't care? Why is it I am left to suffer oblivion and failure while people, whom I don't want to judge but who obviously neglect your rules and even your commandments, bask in the limelight and collect admiration? Why can I, who am your true servant, be left behind in life, while others who are your servants only in name (if at all!) enjoy popularity and thrive all round in society?

But my feet were almost stumbling; my steps had nearly slipped, because I was jealous of the boasters and begrudged the wealth of the wicked. . . . They scoff and speak evil; arrogantly they talk of oppression. They think their mouth is heaven and their tongue can dictate on earth. This is why my people turn to them and sip up all they say, asking, "How will God find out? Does the Most High know everything? Look at them: these are the wicked, well-off and still they increase in riches." After all, why should I keep my own heart pure and wash my hands in innocence if you plague me all day long and discipline me every morning?

That is my temptation, Lord, and I lay it open now before you in the sincerity of my heart. I accept your judgment, I profess my ignorance, I worship the mystery. I know that you are just and that you are merciful, and it is not for me to call you to account or to expect your views to conform to mine. You have time on your side, you love all people, and you know what is best for each at each moment. And you know what is best for me. I see all that; I feel deeply, and I want to strengthen my faith through the contemplation of your action among humankind. You are free to bestow your graces on people, and the good of all is always enshrined in what you do for each one.

Soften in me that urge to compare myself to others, to feel threatened by their successes and belittled by their achievements. Teach me to rejoice with the joy of my brothers and sisters, to smile with their smile, to take as given to me the graces that you give to them. Remind me to respect always your judgments, to wait for your time, to give you the benefit of eternity. And above all, Lord, give me the special grace never to classify people into good and bad, to label them, to throw them with intemperate pride into categories that only my own mind has built. You alone know the human heart, you are Judge and you are Father. Let me love all people as brothers and sisters, and let me free myself from the self-imposed burden of judging others' consciences without knowing them. Let me stay by your side, happy and contented to be where you want me to be.

Now guide me with your counsel and receive me into glory at last. No one else in heaven can attract me; I delight in nothing else on earth.

Psalm 74

There Is No Prophet!

This is the grief of Israel: There is no prophet!

Without signs on our behalf, or prophets to guide us, none of us knows how long this will last.

If we only had a leader, a religious leader like Moses, who would be in contact with God, could tell us his will, could interpret for us our own situation on earth, which makes no sense to us, could make sense out of our sufferings and show with divine authority a direction of hope. If we only had a prophet among us to point out our misdeeds and guide our lives into redemption, we would find resignation in our sorrow, light in our doubts and strength in our path. But there is no prophet; there is no light; there is no hope, and the people of God suffer under the existential uncertainty of their own destiny. Sheep without a shepherd. The sight that brings tears to the eyes of those who love the people.

Have you rejected us forever? Why, O God? Why is your fury burning against the sheep of your pasture? Remember your flock, which you gathered of old, the people you saved as your inheritance—Mount Zion, where you live. Step carefully through these utter ruins, toward all the destruction the enemy has done in the sanctuary.

There is no prophet in your people today, Lord. That is our grief and our sorrow. Yes, there is no lack of well-meaning workers among us, there are organizers and ministers and administrators and officials, and all do their job conscientiously and effectively, and we need them and appreciate them, and all that is very fine and very proper. But we have no prophet. We have no charismatic leadership, no original thinker, no bold pathfinder. We miss Isaiah, Daniel, and John the Baptist. We need them badly. We, ourselves, do our jobs with constancy and fidelity, yes, but rather routinely and dishearteningly. We plod along, and we do our duty, but our eyes are down on the markings of the path instead of looking up to the shining of the stars.

The world needs your presence, Lord, your presence through people who may speak in your name and act with your power. Our youth look up to new models of sanctity; our hearts long for new adventures of evangelical action. We want a place in the world, not just as a respectable organization but as a dynamic leaven in society. We want your hand to be shown in the deep crisis humanity is going through today. Why do you keep silent, Lord?

How much longer, O God, will the enemy blaspheme? Will they slander your name forever? Why stay your hand and stop your right hand—idle under your cloak?

Act, Lord, through the people of your choice. Send prophets to your people; send leaders; send saints. Shake us through their voice into a new awareness of the needs of our world and the ways to meet them with a Christian presence. Your prophets came always from the ranks, from the fields, from the deep faith of humble believers, from the eternal anonymity of the quarries of hope. Sound your call and bring out your people, Lord. Give us the eyes to recognize them and the heart to follow them. Let your prophets revitalize your people again, Lord.

Yet, God, my protector from times past, you bring salvation to the earth. . . . The day and night are yours; you fashioned the sun and the moon. You established the bounds of the land; summer and winter—you make them. . . . Arise, O God, defend your cause; do not forget the endless blaspheming of the fool. Recollect the roaring of your foes, the increasing tumult among your enemies.

You work through your prophets, Lord. Thank you for the prophets of old. Send us new prophets now!

Psalm 75

The Cup of Bitterness

This psalm frightens me, Lord. Your image as a strict Judge with the cup of retribution in your hands, holding it forcibly to the lips of sinners to make them drink the dregs of damnation while no power on earth can save them from your wrath, frightens me.

No power from the east or from the west, no power from the wilderness can raise a person up. For God is judge, who puts one down and raises up another. In the hand of Yahweh there is a cup; the wine foams in it, mixed with spice. Yahweh offers it to everyone for drink, and all the wicked on earth must drink it down to the dregs.

Frightful image of judgment and punishment. Yet I don't want to forget it, Lord, I don't want to pass it by, to gloss it over. Your justice is also part of your being, and I accept it and worship it as I do your mercy and your majesty. You are a just judge, and the cup of retribution is in your hands. Let me never forget that, Lord.

I don't want to claim exemption for myself; in fact I don't dare. I know my wrong deeds, and I know my lips have condemned themselves to touch the brim of the cup of malediction. I cannot hide in east or west or even in the wide wilderness or in the very ends of the earth. I don't want to hide either. I dread the cup, but I trust the hand that holds it. I wait for the coming of the judge.

I wait in hope because I think of another cup, remote in time but not unrelated in content. A cup of bitterness, of suffering, and of death. And that cup was also in your hand in the solitude of a garden where the rays of the full moon filtered shyly through the clustered leaves of olive trees onto a figure that prayed in agony. The cup was full of the dregs of death, and the cup did not pass away. It was drunk to the full. Mystery of the cup in the garden which canceled the cup destined for my lips.

This, O Lord, is the greatness of your mercy and the glory of your redemption. If I have praised you for the heavens and the earth, for the sun and for the moon, I praise you now much more for the greatest of your wonderful works, your redemption of humanity through the life, death, and resurrection of your own Son.

We give you thanks, O God; we give you thanks. Your name is brought very near to us in the story of your wonderful deeds.

Psalm 76

The Scourge of War

As I begin my prayer, Lord, I am reminded that there are wars being waged at this very moment far and near on the face of the earth. Cruel, senseless, inhuman wars. Wars that have been going on for years and wars that have flared up without notice and without reason. There is never reason for a war. There is never reason to shed the blood of those who want to live. There is never reason to ruin nations and foster hatred and drag human history through the shame and the suffering of whole generations of humankind.

Yahweh broke the flashing arrows, the shield, the sword, the weapons of war. You, Yahweh, are dazzling with light—more majestic than the everlasting mountains. The defeated warriors sleep in death; the hands of the soldiers were powerless. At your rebuke, horse and rider lay stunned. You, you alone are to be feared. Who shall stand when your anger is roused? You pronounced your sentence from the heavens.

Make the earth silent again, Lord. Let the earth with its silence acknowledge your dominion, Lord. Let bombs and explosions and mines and bullets cease to crease the face of the earth. Let the tumult of war subside in the human heart and on the fields of battle. Let the silence of peace envelope the earth. Let the songs of birds be heard again instead of the rattle of machine guns. Let weapons be destroyed that they may not destroy human civilization in its own home.

Make silence in my own heart, Lord, because it is there that the sources of war are found. The passions that lead people to seek power, to hate each other, to kill, and to destroy are all present in my heart. Silence violence in me; silence pride, and silence hatred. When I read news of wars it makes me think of the secret wars of my own heart. When I decry violence it reminds me of the seeds of violence within me. When I see blood it brings before my eyes the blood that I shed unseen in the spiteful encounters with my enemies. Silence the storm within that it may never rage outside, and let the peace of my soul be sign and prayer of the peace I want for all people in all places and in all times.

The earth feared and was still when you arose to judge, to save the afflicted of the earth. People's anger will serve to praise you; the survivors surround you in joy.

Make the clamor of battle change into the music of dancing, Lord God of peace!

Psalm 77

The Right Hand of God

Have you forgotten how to be gracious? Have you withheld your compassion in anger? Has your right hand changed? Is the arm of the Most High powerless?

Forgive my vehemence, Lord, but when I think of your power and my miseries, of your promises and my failures, I feel that something is wrong, and I express the frustration of my heart in the despair of my words. Have you failed me, Lord? Have you let me down? Where are all my efforts, my prayers, my hopes? I am the same old wreck I always was, nothing has improved in me, my temper continues to hurt people, my intemperance continues to hurt me, my passions are stronger than ever and my failures multiply with age. Where is your power, your mercy, your grace? Where is the might of your hands? Has your right hand lost its grip? Does your arm hang powerless? Have you lost your influence in human affairs? Have you lost your interest?

I speak for me, and I speak for the friends and companions with whom I share the work of the Kingdom and with whom I speak of the disillusionment that chills us when we compare the earnestness of our efforts with the meagerness of our results.

Yahweh, will you reject us forever and never again show us your favor? Has your unfailing love now failed us completely? Will your promise be unfulfilled?

When the cloud of disappointment sweeps over me I feel discouragement and despair. Dreams are not fulfilled; ideals are not reached; the Kingdom does not arrive. I know my defects, and I know the failings of the human race, but I also know the firmness of your promises and the power of your hand. Don't let your hand rest idle, Lord. The hand that created the world, that opened the sea, that brought down massive walls can now do much more than that, can do work beyond the figure of those material events, can do work in the reality of the lives of human beings and of the welfare of their souls. That is where your marvelous works are to shine, where your right hand has to exert its power.

Lord, let it never be said of you, not even in the obedient question of a devoted friend, that your right hand has lost its grip.

Psalm 78

Salvation History

I know the history, Lord, and I know its lesson. I know that the journey of your chosen people from Egypt to Canaan is a symbol of my own life from birth to death, from sin to redemption, from captivity to liberation. I now relive that story in my heart while I see myself in the telling episodes of the march through the desert.

The story is a poem, and the poem has a theme and a refrain. The theme is your bounty, your care, and your power, always ready to help your people in every difficulty and to supply them in every need. The refrain is the ingratitude of the people who, no sooner than they have received a favor from you, start a new complaint, doubt your power, and shout rebellion. I go on reading the chapters of their pilgrimage, and I go on thinking of the circumstances in my life, which I see mirrored in them. Will I learn the lesson at the end?

You did wonderful deeds in the sight of their ancestors in the land of Egypt, in the region of Zoan. You divided the sea and led them through; you make the water stand firm like a wall. You guided them with the cloud by day and with light from the fire all night.

Those were wonders enough to establish a people's faith forever. Yet their effect did not last long. Yes, God has taken us out of Egypt, but can he give us water in the desert?

You split the rocks in the desert and gave them water as abundant as the seas; you brought streams out of a rocky crag and made water flow down like rivers.

New wonders to strengthen the faith. And yet new doubts and new complaints. Yes, he has given us water; but can he give us bread? Can he give us meat to eat in the desert?

But they continued to sin against you, rebelling in the wasteland against the Most High. They willfully put God to the test by demanding the food they craved. They spoke against you, saying: "Can God spread a table in the desert? When Moses struck the rock, water gushed out, and streams flowed abundantly. But can God also give us bread and supply meat for the people?" . . .

Your wrath rose against Israel; for they did not believe in you or trust in your deliverance. Yet you gave a command to the skies above and opened the doors of the heavens; you rained down manna for the people to eat and gave them the bread of heaven. They ate the bread of the mighty; you sent them more than enough food to eat. You stirred up the east wind from the heavens and led forth the south wind by your power. You rained meat down on them like dust, birds like sand on the seashore. You made birds fall inside their camp, all around their tents. They ate until they had more than enough, for you had given them what they craved. But before they turned from the food they craved—even while it was still in their mouths—your anger rose against them.

That is the story of the fickleness of Israel. Wonder after wonder, and complaint after complaint. Short-lived faith, which believed only for an instant in order to doubt the next. Stiff-necked people unwilling to accept the reality of God's power and God's protection daily shown to them and daily forgotten.

Their hearts were not loyal to you; they were not faithful to your covenant. Yet you were merciful. . . . How often they rebelled against you in the desert and grieved you in the wilderness. Again and again they put you to the test; they provoked the Holy One of Israel.

Dismal story of a stubborn people, and dismal story of my own soul. Have I not experienced enough your power, your protection, your providence? Have I not seen you act in my life, Lord, from the miracle of my birth through the wonders of my youth to the fullness of my maturity? Have you not rescued me from a thousand dangers; have you not fed me with grace in my soul and food in my body; have you not blessed me with the health of nature and the joy of life? Have I not felt your loving presence by my side at every turn of my life in company, warmth, and support? Have you not proved yourself to me time and again as friend, protector, father, and God?

And yet I doubt. I forget. I ignore. I chafe. I complain. You have given me freedom, but can you give me water? Can you give me bread? Can you give me meat? You have called me to the life of the spirit, but can you teach me to pray? Can you give me

144

detachment? Can you raise me to contemplation? Can you control my temper? Can you lift up my moods? Can you give me true faith? Can you give me true happiness? Every grace of yours is followed by a complaint of mine. Every demonstration of your power lands me in a new doubt. Thus far you have done it, but will you be able to do it in the future? You have done much, but can you do everything? Can you make me truly loving, saintly, free, devoted, selfless, committed, healthy, and happy? Can you? And if you can, why don't you show it now and make me into the truly fine person I dream to be?

But they put you to the test and rebelled against the Most High; they did not keep your statutes. Like their ancestors they were disloyal and faithless; they recoiled like a faulty bow. They angered you with their high places; they aroused your jealousy with their idols.

Have patience with me, yet, Lord. Open my eyes to see your works and trust your power. Let the lessons of the past build up my confidence in the future. Revive my memory to keep always before my mind what you have done, in order to feel sure of what you can do. Let me set no limits on your action; let me bring no doubts into our relationship. Let me trust you blindly at any time and for anything. You have done enough to deserve that trust forever. Clear my clouds and shorten my desert. Let me not abuse your patience any more. Let me feel sure that you can cope with any situation and want to do and will do so. Let me give you credit for your record of mercy. Let me proclaim my faith by ceasing to complain about the present and worry about the future. Let me acknowledge in practice that you are the Lord of creation, of Israel, and of my own life by leaving it in your hands without reservation and without a care. I call you Lord, and I want you to be truly Lord of my life by surrendering to you in the totality of my faith and the fullness of my joy. No more complaints from me, Lord.

I know I have suffered for my doubts and my guilt. Let me now find consolation in your pardon to your people in spite of all their infidelities.

Time after time you restrained your anger and did not stir up your wrath. You remembered that they were but flesh, a passing breath that does not return. . . . Thus you brought them to the border of your holy land, to the hill country your right hand had won. You drove out nations before them and gave their lands to them as an inheritance; you settled the tribes of Israel in their homes.

Salvation history has a happy end. Let me anticipate that happiness in my life, Lord.

Psalm 79

The Enemy Within

O God, the nations have invaded your heritage.

I read a modern danger in the ancient alarm. The heathen have set foot in your domain. The secular mind has gained a foothold in religious circles. Rationalism has infiltrated your Church. Authority is played down; dogma is explained away; traditions are ignored; obedience is minimized. Everything is rationalized, secularized, demythologized. A rationalist outlook on religious truth. Reason over faith. Human before God. That is the danger in the religious world today. That is the heathen foothold in the sanctuary of Jerusalem.

And that is the danger in my own life. I live in the midst of the sanctuary, but I am affected by the heathen winds that sweep through it. They all think that way; that is the modern trend; the latest theologians favor that outlook; all scholars now take the liberal interpretation. That is the danger. The assaults from outside the sanctuary are easily rejected because they are recognized for what they are. The cunning insinuations from inside are much more difficult to resist because they look friendly and harmless. Yet their harm is greater as they go unnoticed and strike in the dark.

I want the fullness of the faith, Lord. I want no compromise, no misgivings, no half-truths. I want the sanctuary of my soul to be free from any pagan touch, any heathen influence. I want the integrity of your word and the totality of your revelation. I don't want to jeopardize eternal truths with passing fashions. I want the purity of your sanctuary and the sanctity of your temple. I want the Holy City to remain holy forever. I want my faith to shine without shadows and without flickers. I want to be modern by being traditional, to be actual by being eternal. I want to know the latest research from the firmness of my permanent convictions. I want fidelity to you, Lord, to rule my mind and my life forever.

Restore in your Church the firmness of your revelation. Purify our thoughts and strengthen our beliefs. Cleanse your sanctuary and sanctify your city. Illumine the doctrine of your faithful with the brightness of your truth.

Then we your people, the flock that you pasture, will give you everlasting thanks and will recite your praises forever and ever.

Psalm 80

Prayer for the Church

It gives me joy, Lord, to see that I can address you today in the very words you inspired ages ago, that I can say for your Church today the prayer your psalmist said for your people when your word was made Scripture and every poet was a prophet. I know the image of the vine and its branches and the wall around it and the damage done to that wall and its restoration at your hands. I identify with every word, with every mood, and I pray for your vine today in words that have been familiar to you ever since your people was first called your people.

From Egypt you uprooted a vine; to plant it you scattered other nations. You cleared a space so it could flourish, and it took root and filled the land. Soon it shaded the mountains, the cedars of God by its branches. Its leaves stretched to the sea, its shoots to the river. Why have you leveled its fences? Now all can pluck its fruit. The wild boar can trample it, and wild beasts devour it. O Yahweh, please return! Look down from heaven and see this vine. Nurture and guard what your hand has planted. They tossed it on the flames like rubbish, but your glance would destroy them. Safeguard those you have chosen, those you have made strong. Never again will we turn away from you; we shall call on your holy name with a renewed spirit.

The vine, the boughs, the mountains, the wall. The time of trial and the person of your choice. These are terms of yesterday for realities of today. You inspired the prayer, Lord, and you had it preserved that I could bring it before you today. You like to listen to those words because you want to do what you move us to ask you in prayer. With that confidence I pray, and I enjoy doubly this prayer in which I can use inspired words of another age to urge vital needs of my present day.

Restore us, Yahweh Sabaoth; let your face smile on us—then we will be safe.

Psalm 81

Remember Your Liberation

I am Yahweh, your God, who brought you up from Egypt.

A people that forgets its origins loses its identity. That is why God's great commandment to Israel is: Remember Egypt! Only then will you remember the Lord who brought you out of Egypt, and you will be his people and he will be your God.

What makes us a people is our common origin in Christ, our liberation, our redemption. We too were slaves, though we do not like to remember that. We take for granted our independence and our freedom, our human progress and social welfare; we take all that as normal and natural and due to us, and in the process we lose the common bonds that bind us to each other and to God. We have forgotten Egypt, and we have ceased to be a people.

For this is a law for Israel, a decree of the God of Abraham and Sarah, laid as a solemn charge on Joseph when he came out of Egypt.

Remember your past, remember your origins, remember your liberation. Remember Bethlehem and Jerusalem and Mount Calvary. Remember, deep in your personal history, your own bondage under passions and vices and sin. Remember the personal slavery and universal captivity from which we were redeemed by the salvific action that made us one in Christ. That is our common root, our single history, our radical unity. Memory makes us one, while forgetfulness scatters us into separate groups and opposed factions. A person without a memory is no longer a person. A people without a history is no longer a people.

Give me the grace of memory, Lord. Make me recall; make me remember; make me be mindful. Let me have always before my eyes the poverty of my lowliness and the splendor of your redemption. You broke my chains; you tamed my vices; you healed my wounds; you uplifted my spirits. You gave me new life, Lord, and in that new life is expressed my new identity as a member of your chosen people. I too have come out of Egypt, and I have not come out alone but in the midst of a joyous crowd that felt the same liberation because they all had been under the same yoke.

To be truly myself I want to feel a member of your people. I accept your commandment to remember, and I ask for the grace to fulfill it so as to build the hopes of my future on the firmness of my past. I am one with your people, one in liberation, one in hope, and one in the end in fulfillment forever.

Yes, you are the Lord my God who has brought me out of Egypt.

Psalm 82

Judge of Judges

Justice on earth is not justice any more, Lord. Humankind has corrupted its ways, and those who had to take your place to settle disputes and bring peace among all people, have betrayed their trust and have yielded to the common tide of self-interest before impartial justice. The courts of liberation have at times become the quarters of oppression. The poor seek redress in the halls of justice, and their burden increases when they seek to be delivered from it. Humankind suffers from lack of honesty in those who should exhibit it most.

"How long will you defend the unjust and favor the cause of the wicked?" Defend the poor and the orphaned; render justice to the afflicted and the oppressed. Rescue the lowly and the poor; from the clutches of the wicked deliver them. They have neither knowledge nor understanding—they walk about blindly. All the order of the world is shaken.

For the sake of the oppressed I pray for justice, Lord. Give courage to your judges, make them recognize innocence, denounce guilt, and deliver their sentence without fear. Make them give confidence to your people and kindle a ray of hope in a society that has lost its sense of fairness and equity. Let there be justice on earth as a sign and pledge of your divine justice in heaven.

Rise, O God; judge the earth, for yours are all the nations.

Psalm 83

Time for Action

O God, do not be silent; do not hold your peace or keep still, O God!

You are an active God, Lord; that is the way I have known you from the days of creation to the care of your people and your walking with them on earth and inspiring them through your Spirit in the initiative of your directives and the power of your help. You were cloud and column of fire; you were storm and wind; you opened up seas and brought down walls; you led armies and won battles; you called people and ruled kingdoms; you inspired virtue and made martyrdom possible. Yours was the greatest power in the world, Lord, and the people knew it and acknowledged it with awe.

Now, on the contrary, you seem to keep quiet. The world goes round by itself, and your presence is not felt. People do what they please, and nations go their own way without any reference to you. And you keep quiet. No bright cloud and no column of fire are to be seen now. No trumpets of Jericho and no winds of Pentecost. You do not count; you are ignored; you are silent. Have you given us up, Lord?

And when I think of my own life I find the same situation. There was a time when I felt your presence and experienced your power. You spoke to me; you inspired me; you led me. It was in the enthusiasm of my youth and the fervor of my growing years, but you were to me as real as my closest friend, and you took part in my plans and my decisions, in my joys and in my sorrows, with a daily realism of faith and experience. Now for a long time you have been silent. I don't hear your voice; I don't feel your presence. You are just absent from my life, and, yes, I go on doing the things I always did and believing the things I always believed, but I do this out of habit, out of routine, without conviction and without zest. When I speak of experiencing you I speak of the past, when I extol your graces and your power I speak from memory. You have faded from my experience; you are silent in my life.

Speak again, O Lord. Make yourself again actual and real to me and to all people who love your coming. Take your rightful place in the world you have created and in my heart, which is still yours. Silence those who ignore you, discount you, or neglect you. Break your silence and let the world know that you are here and you are in charge.

Let them know that you alone are God, whose name is the Most High over all the earth.

Psalm 84

Love of God's Temple

How I love your dwelling place, Yahweh Sabaoth!

When I say these lovely words, Lord, I think of a number of things at once in my mind, and several images surge in happy confusion from the depths of my memory. I imagine the Temple of Jerusalem, stately cathedrals I have seen, and small chapels I have prayed in. I think of the temple of my heart, of the visions of the book of Revelation, and of paintings of heaven—whatever can be called your house, your temple, your dwelling place. All that is dear to me and becomes the aim of my desires and the focus of my longing.

Happy those who dwell in your house and praise you all day long.

I know that your house is the whole world, that you fill every space and are present in every heart. But I also like the symbol, the image, and the sacrament of your holy temple where I feel almost physically near you, where I can visit you, worship you, and kneel before you in the sacred intimacy of your own house.

Only one day in your courts is worth more than a thousand elsewhere.

In the secret of my mind, in the freedom of my fantasy, in the reality of my pilgrimages, in the devotion of my visits I see myself kneeling before your altar, which is your presence, your throne, your home. I enjoy being there with my body whenever I can and with my imagination whenever I desire. I seek a place for me in your home, a corner in your temple.

Finally, the sparrow has found its home, the swallow a nest for its young—your altars, Yahweh Sabaoth, O my God.

Just to be there, to feel at home near you, to be surrounded by memories that speak of you, to be penetrated by the smell of incense, to sing sacred hymns that I have known since childhood, to witness the majesty of your liturgy, to bow in unison with your people before the secret certainty of your presence, is enough. That is joy in my heart and strength to live my life wherever it may be, with the thought of your temple always before me.

I feel at home in your house, Lord. Will you feel at home in my house too? Come to my heart. Let our visits be mutual, our contact renewed, our familiarity grow through frequent meetings in your place and in mine. Let my heart, too, become your temple in the glow of your presence and the permanence of your memory. And let your temple become my home in the length of my visits and the longing during my absences.

How my soul yearns and pines for your courts! . . . Yahweh Sabaoth, happy those who put their trust in you.

Psalm 85

Justice and Peace

I will hear what you, God, proclaim: a voice that speaks of peace—
peace for your faithful and those who turn to you in hope.

Peace is your blessing, Lord, on the human heart and on the
race of the earth. Human beings at peace with themselves, with
each other, with the whole of creation, and with you, their Master
and Lord. Peace that is health in the mind and wholeness in the
body, unity in the family and prosperity in society. Peace that
unites, reconciles, heals, and gives joy. Peace that is the greeting of
people to each other in all languages of the world, the motto of
their organizations and the slogan of their public meetings. Peace
that is easy to invoke and hard to achieve. Peace that, in spite of an
announcement by angels, has never quite arrived on earth, never
quite settled in my heart.

Love and faithfulness have met; justice and peace have embraced.

The condition of peace is justice. Justice that gives all their
due between person and person and justice that justifies the failings of humanity with the forgiving mercy of God. If I want peace
in my soul I must learn to be fair to all those with whom I live and
about whom I speak, and if I want peace in society I must strive
for social justice in the structures of society and in the relationships between classes and between people. It is only justice that
will bring abiding peace to our troubled earth.

The biblical word for the good person is "just." In justice I
fulfill my duty to God, to myself, and to all people. In justice I find
the sensitivity to recognize all people as brothers and sisters and
give all their due with joyful readiness and open generosity. I
must find justice even in my words, which tend to be unfair and
disparaging when I speak of others, and justice even in my
thoughts, which only too easily condemn the behavior of others in

the private court of my own mind. When justice is found in these places, justice will emerge in my conduct and my dealings with all, and I will be "just," as I desire to be.

Justice in my own life will then give me the right to proclaim justice for others in the public forum, which is fraught with injustices and where oppression rears its head. I will then have the right to proclaim equality, openness, fairness for everybody and in everything. I will develop an awareness of the deep cleft between classes and peoples and with the awakening, both emotional and practical, to the urgency of the cause of justice for the very survival of humankind.

Justice then will bring peace—peace in my soul to balance my emotions, my feelings, my joys, and my sorrows in the equanimity of the heavenly perspective of things; and peace in the world to make a reality the divine gift God brought with him when he came to dwell among humankind. Justice and peace are the blessing that accompany the Lord wherever he goes.

Yahweh, you will give what is good, and our earth shall yield its fruit. Justice shall march before you, and peace shall follow your steps.

Psalm 86

Guide Me, O Lord!

Teach me your way, Yahweh, and I will obey you faithfully; give me an undivided heart that I may fear your name.

Today I ask for guidance, Lord. I feel so confused at times, so helpless when I have to make up my mind and put aside an option and take another, that I have come to realize it is my lack of contact with you that makes me lose clarity and feel perplexed when I come to make decisions in my life. I pray for the grace to be near you so that I may see with your light and be strengthened by your support when I make the choices that steer my life.

At times it is external factors that confuse me: what people say, the way they talk, pressures on me, prejudices, atmosphere, fashions, and slogans. I don't know where I stand, and I find it impossible to define myself and see clearly and go straight. Clear up the air round me, Lord, that I may see far and recognize my goals.

Deeper in me is the confusion I feel inside, the fears, the attachments, the lack of freedom, the cloud of selfishness. It is there that I especially need your presence and your help, Lord. Free me from all complexes in me that prevent me from making the right choices. Give me balance; give me wisdom; give me peace. Temper my moods, and tame my instincts that I may be impartial in my own cause and choose the right way without impediment.

Guide me in the important choices of my life and in the passing options that make up the routine of the day and that, step by step, mark the direction in which my life moves. Train me in the small options that I may confidently tackle the big ones. Direct each step of mine that the whole way may be straight and may lead me where you want me to go.

Teach me your way, Yahweh, and I will obey you faithfully.

Psalm 87

Zion, Mother of Peoples

"Zion is called 'Mother' since all were born in her."

The boundaries of my heart are enlarged, Lord, when I say this and when I dream of that moment. Children of every race come together because all have become one in you. This is your own plan, and I embrace it with open faith and keen desire. All races are one. All humankind meet. All are children of the same mother. The moment of unity toward which we move. The seal of brother- and sisterhood. The supreme destiny of the human race.

"Of Philistia, Tyre, Ethiopia, people say, 'Here so and so was born.' But Zion is called 'Mother,' since all were born in her."

All nations are born in the Holy City. All people are my fellows. I look at their faces and I recognize in them the family traits under the joyful variety of features and colors. I project into each face the feeling of fellowship and recognition that grows over me while I look at the person. I feel bonded in birth to each man and woman, and I trust my own conviction to shine through my eyes and to vibrate in my words to carry the family message in the waves of my faith.

No frontiers, no boundaries, no exclusions. No one is a stranger to another. Nature abhors bureaucracy. Bonds of birth transcend impositions of legislation. Unity is our birthright. Our smile is our passport. With it we have freedom to travel, freedom to meet, freedom to face any human being and feel one with him or her, and courage to forget our differences and recognize our common destiny. We all are children of Zion.

Give me a truly ecumenical heart, Lord. Let me love every person and respect all peoples. Let me feel at home in every culture, love to learn, and grow to understand. Let me discover your presence in the hearts of all people and learn your name in all languages. Let me strengthen my roots and deepen my sources with the faith that in doing that I am coming closer to my fellow human beings because all our sources are in you.

And all shall sing and dance! All find their home in you.

Psalm 88

Loneliness, Sickness, and Death

You have turned my friends against me and made me a pariah to them. . . . You have turned my friends and neighbors against me; now darkness is my only friend.

The burden of loneliness is heavy upon me. I feel alone in the world. There is no one I can call mine, no one I can feel near. I see the crowds, and I move among people, but they are all strangers in an unfriendly world. I see no faces; I hear no greetings. Humankind is in a hurry, and each ignores each in a frenzied activity of meaningless hustle. I am surrounded by people, but I feel no warmth. I talk to others, but I make no contact. They say that in the future robots will replace people. Haven't they done so already?

You have plunged me to the bottom of the pit, into its very bottom. I am crushed by your anger, drowned beneath your waves.

I feel abandoned, alone, let down. All my hopes have been crushed into nothingness. All my dreams have turned into despair. I repeat prayers that always meant much to me, and today they sound hollow; I pronounce the sacred name of God, but it dies on my lips. Nothing helps; nothing makes sense. There is only darkness and emptiness. Passivity and apathy. Sickness and death.

I am counted among those who, without strength, go down to the pit. I am alone, down among the dead, among the slain in their graves— among those you have forgotten, those deprived of your care.

I have no will to live, and I have no courage to die. Death frightens me with the black unknown of what lies beyond the grave. When my faith shone bright I enjoyed life and braved death, because life with faith was walking towards you, Lord, and death in faith was finding you. Now my faith is under a cloud, and I resent life and fear death. What awaits me after that dreadful moment? If I am not sure of myself in this life, how can I be sure in the next? If my existence here has become a burden, what will it become in the Realm of Shadows?

Are your wonders meant for the dead? Can they rise up to praise you? Who proclaims your love from the grave, your faithfulness among those who have died? Are your wonders discussed in the dark, your justice in the land of oblivion?

Where are you sending me, Lord, when I depart from the only existence I know, miserable though it is? Is it to the *land of oblivion?* Is my existence to be a transit from nothingness to nothingness? Am I less than the birds that entrust their wings to the sky, less than the flowers that have at least their day of glory in the gaiety of their colors? Do I count for nothing in your sight? Are you simply watching with indifference the anguish of my soul?

O God, why do you reject me? Why do you hide your face from me? I am afflicted and have suffered since my youth; I bore your fury; now I almost despair. Your anger overwhelmed me; you shattered me with your terrors, which, like flood, engulfed me all day long—all together closing in on me.

This is the story of my sufferings, Lord, and there is no one to whom I would tell them except you. See my latent faith in my very complaints, my trust in you in the freedom with which I speak to you. I wouldn't have dared to speak thus to you if you had not put the words in my mouth. Thank you for giving me that freedom, Lord. Thank you for your psalm, which is yours in the inspiration of your word and mine in the agony of my experience. Shorten now my trial and restore me to life.

May my prayer come to you. Hear my cries for help, for my soul is troubled; my life draws near to Sheol.

Psalm 89

The Power and the Promise

The psalm is long, but the prayer is short. The long poem softens the sharpness of the pointed appeal. I feel enough confidence with you, Lord, to make first the appeal in all its bluntness, and then to go and lengthen it in the poetry of the psalm. Few psalms touch me more deeply than this one, Lord.

The appeal is clear and definite. You are powerful, Lord, powerful in the skies you have made and in the earth you have created. No one can resist you, and if you choose not to do something it is not for lack of power. You are also faithful and keep the promises you have made. You made a promise to David that his descendants would rule Israel forever, and you specified that your promise would stand even if the descendants proved not worthy. You declared that David's throne would be firm in Israel as the sun and the moon in the sky. And I know well that Israel is your Church and that David is a figure of Jesus. Well then, Lord: The sun and the moon are still there, but David's throne is no more. Jerusalem is destroyed, and Israel is defeated. Why?

I will sing the wonders of your love forever, Yahweh; I will proclaim your faithfulness to all generations. I will declare that your love is steadfast, your faithfulness fixed as the heavens.

Nice beginning for a frontal attack, isn't it? Did you guess, Lord, what was coming in this psalm after this beautiful opening? Your love is firm and your fidelity eternal. Surely you love to hear that. Sincere praise from the people who knew you best. And on a point you are sensitive about, too: your faithfulness. Your truth that never fails and your promises that never disappoint. But from this moment you are caught, Lord, by the very words you like to hear. You are faithful, and you keep your promises. Why, then, have you not kept your solemn promise to your people and your king?

The heavens praise your wonders, Yahweh. . . . In the skies who is there like Yahweh? . . . O God of Hosts, who is like you? Your strength and faithfulness surround you. You rule the surging sea, calming the turmoil of its waves. . . . Yours are the heavens; the earth is yours also. You founded the world with all that is in it. . . . Strength of arm and power are yours. Your hand is mighty, your right hand lifted high. Your throne is built upon righteousness and justice; true love and faithfulness herald your coming.

The rhythm of praise continues. For your power and your strength, for your dominion over land and sea. Everybody acknowledges these things from the angels in heaven to the people on earth. Nothing can resist you. You are the lord of history, the master of the human heart. You ordain events and dispose circumstances just as you establish mountains and orbit stars. All is the work of your hands. We have seen you at work, and we recognize your sovereignty over all that is. We are proud of being your people because there is no god like you, Lord.

Happy the people who have learned to acclaim you, who walk in the light of your presence! . . . You are their strength and glory; and by your favor we hold our heads high. Yahweh is our shield; the Holy One of Israel is our ruler.

Your power is our guarantee. Your strength is our boast. We are happy to be the people whose God you are. We rejoice in your glory and love to retell the story of your wonderful deeds. Your history is our history, and your Spirit is our life. Our destiny on earth as a people is the expression of your divine will, and so we extoll your will and venerate your majesty. You are our God, and we are your people.

And now comes the promise. Wide and generous, firm and immovable. We like to remember every word, to savor every phrase, to witness your solemn oath, and to treasure in our memory the charter of our future. A promise that is strength to our heart and music to our ears.

I have sworn to my servant David: I will establish his posterity forever, I will make his throne firm for all generations. . . . I have found David my servant: I have anointed him with my holy oil. My hand shall be ready to help him, and my arm to give him strength. . . . My faithfulness and true love shall be with him, and through my name he shall hold his head high. . . . I will maintain my love for him forever and be faithful in my covenant with him. I will make his posterity last forever and his throne as long as the heavens endure.

These are consoling words from one who is truth itself. Only the nagging doubt remains: If we fail you, if your people prevaricates, if the king proves unworthy of the throne, will that not invalidate the promise and rescind the covenant? And here come the reassuring words from your own mouth.

If his descendents forsake my law and do not conform to my judgments, if they renounce my statutes and do not observe my commands, I will punish their disobedience with the rod and their iniquity with lashes. Yet I will not deprive them of my true love nor let my faithfulness prove false; I will not renounce my covenant nor change my promise. I have sworn by my holiness once and for all; I will not break my word. His posterity shall continue forever, his throne shall be the sun before me, it shall be sure forever as the moon that remains forever faithful as long as the skies remain.

Divine words of infinite comfort. We may fail you, but you will never fail us. If we misbehave we shall bear the punishment, but God's promise will never be broken; the throne will remain safe and David's descendants on it. The oath is sacred and will remain firm forever. The word of him who made heaven and earth has been pledged on our behalf. Our future is safe.

And yet . . .

Yet you have rejected David and you have spurned and raged against the anointed. You have denounced the covenant with your servant, defiled the crown and flung it to the ground. . . . You have put an end to the glorious rule and hurled the throne to the ground. You have cut short youth and vigor and covered the anointed with shame.

Shame is all that is left to us. We are your people; your Anointed is your Son and our Lord; his throne is the place he holds in the hearts of humankind and in the ruling of society. But society is not very mindful of your Son today, Lord. There is distant respect and polite regard, but little obedience, scant reverence, and limited acceptance. Humankind does not accept your King, Lord, and his throne is not universal. We suffer to see his law disregarded and his person ignored. We are pained to see that things do not seem to improve; on the contrary, people drift farther and farther away from your Kingdom, and we do not know how long this will last.

How long, O God, will you hide yourself from sight? How long must your wrath blaze like fire? . . . Where are the former acts of your love, O God—those faithful promises given to David? Remember the insults hurled at your servant, how I have borne in my heart the accusations of the nations. So have your enemies taunted us, O God, taunted the successors of your anointed one.

And there the psalm ends in abrupt eloquence. There is only a blessing and an Amen tagged on at the end, but that is only the rubric added to mark the end of the Third Book of Psalms. The psalm as such ends in the sudden pain of the taunts that we bear. The next word is yours, Lord.

Book IV

Psalm 90

Life Is Short

Make us realize the shortness of life that we may gain wisdom of heart.

I bring before my eyes a fact of life: life is short. Time passes swiftly. My days are numbered, and that number is not very high. Before I realize it, before I want it, before I can accept it, my day will come, and the moment of my departure is inexorable. So soon? So early? In the flower of my life? When I had still so much to do? Death is always sudden because never expected. It always comes too soon, because it is never welcome.

And yet there is wisdom in the memory of death. When I learn that my days are counted, I am moved to use them well. When I accept that my time is limited, I begin to get the most of it. Life can be revalued by the memory of death.

Our years die away like a murmur. Seventy years is the span of our life, eighty if our strength holds; the hurrying years are labor and sorrow, so quickly they pass and are forgotten.

I accept the shortness of my life, Lord, and in the wisdom of that acceptance I find the strength and the urge to make the best, in humility, of whatever days will be mine. When suffering comes I will know that it will soon pass, and when pleasures beckon I will reflect that they, too, will be with me only for a short time. Thus I will bear suffering and enjoy pleasure with the light heart of one who knows that nothing lasts long. That will bring balance, detachment, and wisdom to my life.

People are like a dream at daybreak; they fade like grass that springs up with the morning but when evening comes is parched and withered.

Let the grass behave like grass. In that lies its happiness. If it's one day it's one day, but let that day be green with the luscious glory of the smiling fields. If my life is to be like grass, let it be green; let it be fresh; let it live in the intensity of the unique morning all the fullness of nature and all the fullness of grace. Each moment now acquires value of eternity, each blade of grass shines with the tender dew under the rising sun. Each instant is revalued; each event is enhanced; each meeting is a surprise; each meal is a feast. The briefness of the experience brings to it the sharpness of pure awareness and free enjoyment. Life becomes precious precisely because it is short.

Give me, Lord, the wisdom to live the fullness of my life in every instant of it.

Psalm 91

God's Daily Care

With pinions God will cover you, and under God's wings you shall find refuge.

All my day is under your care, Lord, and I want to be mindful of it minute by minute as I live my life by day and by night.

You will not fear the terror of the night nor the arrow that flies by day; not the pestilence that stalks in darkness nor the plague that destroys at noon.

By day and night, at noon and in darkness you are with me, Lord. I need that confidence to brave the dangers that beset me. This world is an unsafe place for mind and for body, and I cannot venture alone into the constant threat. I want to hear again the words of reassurance as I start a new day or as I entrust my body to sleep, to feel safe in work and in rest under your loving and unfailing care.

No harm shall befall you, nor shall affliction come near your tent; God has commanded angels to guard you in all your ways. In their hands they shall raise you up so that you will not hurt your foot against a stone.

Lovely words for me. Lovely thought of angels watching my step and saving me from stumbling on a stone. Lovely image of your providence made into wings to flutter over me with the message of your love and your concern. Thank you for your angels, Lord. Thank you for your care of me. Thank you for your love.

Now I want to hear from your own lips the most beautiful words I've ever heard, with the message of your daily care as a sign of the fullness of salvation. Say them slowly, Lord, as I listen to them with all my heart.

"Because you cling to me, I will deliver you; I will protect you because you acknowledge my name. You shall call upon me and I will answer you. I will be with you in times of trouble; I will deliver you and glorify you and will show you my salvation."

Thank you, Lord.

Psalm 92

A Song of Optimism

I wish all days were like today, Lord. I feel light and happy, full of faith and full of energy. I feel sorry for all those complaints, remonstrances, and even accusations I made against you in moments of anger. I don't understand how I can have been so blind to your presence and so forgetful of your graces. It is true that I pass through dark moments at times, but then I have also glorious days like this one in which the sun shines and the birds sing and I want to tell everybody about the happiness I have found in you, which is the greatest a human being can ever find on earth.

O Yahweh, it is good to give you thanks, to sing psalms to your name, O Most High; to declare your love in the morning and your faithfulness every night, with the music of a ten-stringed lute, to the melody of the harp. Your acts, O Yahweh, fill me with gladness; I shout in triumph at your mighty deeds. How great are your deeds, Yahweh! How deep are your thoughts!

Only song and music can do justice to my mood today, Lord. To sing of your greatness, to proclaim at the top of my voice how great you are and how loving you are and how wonderful it is to be in your service and to form part of your people. Oh, when will all people see what I see; when will all come to you and drink at the sources of your grace the happiness that you alone can give? If they only knew your sweetness and your power! How can I tell them, Lord? How can I make my happiness reach others? How can I let all people know that you are the Lord and that in you we all find our rest?

I don't want to preach; I don't want to argue with anyone. I just want to live the happiness you give me today and to let others see the genuineness of my joy. My cheerfulness is my witness. My satisfaction is my messenger.

I lift my head high, like a wild ox tossing its horns; I am anointed with fine oils. . . . The just flourish like a palm tree, they grow tall as a cedar of Lebanon. Planted as they are in the house of the Creator, they flourish in the courts of our God, bearing fruit in old age like trees full of sap—vigorous, wide-spreading—eager to declare that Yahweh is just, my Rock, in whom there is no wrong.

This is my happy mood today. Thanks for it, Lord, long or short as it may prove to be, and be assured from now on of my acceptance from your hands of whatever other mood you may be pleased to send me next.

You, Yahweh, are exalted forever.

Psalm 93

The Lord of the Sea

I watch in awe the eternal sight of the mighty waves of an enraged sea pounding away on the stubborn rocks of the haughty waterfront. The rumbling noise, the heaving tide, the head-on crash, the white fury, the unyielding stand, the foam, the spray, the waters receding in order to come charging again. I never tire of watching the might of the sea, the primeval abyss where life was formed, the secret depth, the untiring breath, the infinite expanse. Figure and mirror of the Lord who made it.

The seas have lifted up, O Yahweh, the seas have lifted up their voice; the seas have lifted up their pounding waves. More powerful that the thunder of the great waters, mightier than the breakers of the sea— Yahweh is powerful on high.

I worship your power, Lord; I bow in humility before your might. In my heart I rejoice to see glimpses of your omnipotence, to see you as unchallenged Master of sea and earth, because I fight on your side, and your victories are mine. I grow in confidence; I acquire courage; I experience joy. My King is the King of kings and Lord of lords. My daily life is easier because you are Lord. My future is safe because you rule all time. My salvation is assured because you, almighty God, are my Redeemer.

I like to look at the sea because it reminds me of your majesty, Lord.

O God, you reign; you are robed in splendor and clothed with strength.

Psalm 94

Teach Me, Lord

Yahweh, happy are those you instruct, those you teach by your law.
I need your instruction, Lord. I want to be a docile pupil in your wide classroom. I want to observe, I want to assimilate, I want to learn. I know that the teaching goes on the whole day, only my learning fails because I do not pay attention; I do not recognize the situations; I do not hear your voice.

Teach me through the events of the day. You put them before me, therefore you know their meaning and their importance for me. Teach me how to read them, how to decipher your messages in a chance encounter, in a piece of news, in a sudden joy, in a threatening worry. You are there, Lord. Your hand is in those writings. Your face is behind those faces. Let me recognize it. Let me understand what you want to tell me through each one of those events and encounters along my day.

Teach me through the silence of my heart. You need no words and no actions. You are present in my moods, and you read my innermost thoughts. Teach me to know myself. Teach me to understand this mess of feelings and this tangle of ideas that is inside me and that I myself don't understand. Why do I react as I react? Why do I feel sad without motive? Why do I get angry with people I love? Why can't I pray when I want to pray? Why do I doubt you when I swear by you? Why do I hate myself when I know you love me? Why am I such a riddle to myself that the more I reflect the less I understand my own mind?

Teach me through others, teach me through experience; teach me through life. Free my instincts from routine and prejudice that they may guide me with nature's wisdom through the jungle of decisions. Enliven my senses that they may give back to me the freshness of creation through the friendliness of my body. Still my mind that it may perceive in virginal innocence the unspoiled images of the world of thought. Cleanse my heart that it may beat with steady confidence to the eternal rhythms of friendship and love.

Teach me through your presence, your word, your grace. Make me see things as you see them; make me value what you value and reject what you reject. Make me trust your Providence and believe that people are good even when they hurt me or wish me ill. Make me have faith in your action among all people and rejoice with the hope of the coming of your Kingdom.

Teach me, Lord; teach me day by day; teach me through my life that I may grow in understanding of myself, of life, and of you and that the light in my mind may illumine the path that leads to you.

Psalm 95

God's Own Rest

"They shall not enter into my rest."

Those are among the most frightful words I have ever heard from you, Lord. The curse of curses. The eternal separation from you. The prohibition to enter your rest. When I reflect on the depth and the beauty of the word "rest"—when it refers to **your** rest—I begin to understand what misery it must be to be excluded from it.

Your rest is your satisfaction after completing the creation of heaven and earth and man and woman on it, your enforced Sabbath of joy and liturgy in the midst of a life of toil, your eternity in the blissful fruition of your being forever. Your rest is the best in you, the leisure of life, the graciousness of mercy, the celebration of your essence in the midst of your creation. Your rest is your smile, your relaxation, your pardon. Your rest is your divine quality of doing everything while seeming to do nothing. Omnipotence without effort, action without fatigue. Your rest is your essence without change in the midst of a world that turns on change. Your rest is you.

And your rest now is open to me. I am called to the eternal holiday. Invited to your heaven. Destined to be with you forever. That magic word "rest" has now become my favorite, with its biblical ring and its theological undertones. A rest so big that one enters into it. It envelops me; it grasps me; it fills me with its bliss. I see easily that such a rest is my final destiny, a homely yet divine word for the ultimate aim of my life: to rest with you.

I want to train myself in this life for the rest in the next. I want to enter already in promise and in spirit the heavenly rest that one day will be mine with you. I want to learn how to be relaxed, to feel at ease, to conquer hurry, to avoid tension, to be at peace. I ask for an anticipation of your blessing, for a pledge on earth of your eternal rest in heaven. I want to reflect in my behavior, my speech, and my countenance the hope of the essential rest that will give my soul and my body the ultimate fruition of perpetual peace.

What prevents me from entering your rest? What led you to swear in your anger, *They shall not enter into my rest?*

"Do not harden your hearts as at Meribah, as on that day in the desert of Massah where your ancestors challenged me; they tested me though they had seen my works."

The incidents remained so sharp in your memory that you quote the very names of the places where they took place, unhappy stages of a spiritual geography that your people lived and that we repeat in our lives. Your people tempted you, mistrusted you even after seeing your wonders, and were stubborn in their complaints and unbelief. Your wrath was kindled, and you closed the door to those who had so long refused to enter.

"Forty years with that generation, and I said: They are a people of erring heart and they know not my ways. Therefore I swore in my anger: They shall not enter into my rest."

How many years for me, Lord? How many chances, how many doubts, how many Massahs and Meribahs? You know the names of my own private geography. You remember my infidelities and regret my stubbornness. Make me docile, Lord. Make me accept; make me believe. Make me see that the way to attain your rest is to trust in you, to rely on you, to put my whole life in your hands with confidence and joy. Then I can live without a care and die in your arms and enter your peace forever. Make it so, Lord.

O that today you would hear God's voice.

Psalm 96

A New Song

Sing Yahweh a new song!

This is, at first sight, an impossible precept. How can I sing a new song when all songs in all languages have already been sung time and time again to you, Lord? All themes are exhausted; all rhymes have been tried; all tunes have been explored. Prayer is essentially repetition, and I must struggle not to appear to say the same things every day, even when I know I am saying the same things. I am condemned to attempt variety even when I know well that all prayer reduces itself to the repetition of your name and the manifestation of my needs. How can you, then, ask me to sing a new song?

I know the answer before I finish the question. The song may be the same, but the spirit with which I sing it must be fresh and new every time. The zest, the joy, the sound of each word and the flight of each note has to be different every time that note leaves my lips, every time that prayer leaves my heart.

This is the secret of newness in life, and in asking me to sing a new song you want to teach me to live a new life each day and each moment with all the freshness of dawn in every minute of my existence. A new song, a new life, a new dawn, a new breath, a new strength behind each step, a new hope behind each thought. Everything the same and everything different, because the eyes that look at the same object of yesterday are new today.

This new sight renders me able to enjoy the blessings of nature in the fullness of their new reality. Heaven and earth and fields and trees become all new because my heart is new. They join me in my joy and sing with me the new song of praise.

Let the heavens be glad, and the earth rejoice; let the sea and all that it holds resound. Let the fields and all that is in them exult; let all the forests cry out for joy at the presence of Yahweh, for God comes to judge the earth, to judge the world with justice and the nations with truth.

This is the new song that fills my life and fills the world around me, the only song that is worthy of him whose essence is to be new each instant in the unrepeatable richness of his eternal being.

Sing Yahweh a new song! Sing to Yahweh, you lands! Sing to Yahweh; bless God's name. Proclaim God's salvation day after day.

Psalm 97

Rejoice in the Lord!

Yahweh, you reign! Let the earth rejoice; let the many coastlands be glad!

The great commandment: "Rejoice!" is sum and substance of all the other commandments. Love and worship; be fair and kind; help others and do good. In a word, rejoice and make others rejoice. Bring to your life and show on your face the happiness that comes from serving the Lord. Rejoice with all your heart in his service. Be sincere in your smile and genuine in your laughter. Achieve joy in your life, and that will be the sign and the proof that you are happy with God and with his creation, happy with other people and with society, and that is the Law and the Prophets. Rejoice and be glad. The Lord is with you.

Zion hears and is glad, and the cities of Judah rejoice because of your judgments, O God.

That is the law of Zion and the rule of Judah. Rejoice and be glad. In that will you show that the Lord is your God and you are his people. Joy as persons and joy as a group. The way to grow, the secret to be strong, the call to all people to witness and reflect on the choice of Israel and the power of his God. The power to make his people rejoice.

It is a difficult virtue, this virtue of joy. Difficult because it has to be genuine and deep, and it is not easy to obtain genuine and deep joy in a world of sorrow. I need faith, Lord, I need a long view and a lasting patience; I need a sense of humor and a light mood, and above all I need the assurance that deep down in me, through all the trials and the sufferings in my private life and in the history of humankind, you are there in the fullness of your power and the tenderness of your love. With that faith I can live, and with that faith I can smile. The gift to rejoice is the flower of your grace in my willing heart.

Thank you for the joy you give me, Lord; thank you for the courage to smile, for the right to hope, for the privilege to look at the world and be glad. Thank you for your love, your power, and your providence, which are the unshakable foundations of my daily joy. Rejoice with me, all you who know and love the Lord.

Rejoice in Yahweh, O you just, and give thanks to God's holy name!

Psalm 98

A Song of Victory

Yahweh has made salvation known, has shown justice to the nations.

I believe in your victory, Lord, as though it had arrived already, and I fight for it on the battlefield as though it still had to be won by your might and my effort. That is the paradox of my life: to have tension at times but certitude always. You have proclaimed your victory in the face of the whole world, and I believe your word and spread your proclamation with total confidence in the face of all doubts and all attacks. You are Lord, and victory is yours. Still, Lord, in all sincerity, your much-heralded victory has not yet appeared, and my faith is on trial. That is my test.

I proclaim victory with my lips and fight for it with my hands. I celebrate the triumph, and I labor to make it come. I believe in the future, and I struggle in the present. I rejoice when I think of the final day, and I shudder when I face the task of today. I know that I belong to a victorious army that in the end will defeat all opposition and conquer the whole world, but I fall in the field of battle with blood on my body and languor in my soul. I am a wounded soldier in a triumphant army. Mine is the triumph and mine are the wounds. Think of me, Lord, when you announce your victories.

Strengthen my faith and open my eyes to make me realize that your victory is already here, though hidden under the humble veil that hides the glory of all heavenly realities while we are on earth. Your victory is here because you are here; you have walked the earth and spoken the human language; you have experienced human plight and proclaimed and effected human redemption; you have tasted death and restored life. I know all that, and I now want to make it all real in my own life and as a witness for others. Make me taste your victory in my soul, that I may proclaim it with my lips.

Meanwhile I rejoice seeing in dream and prophecy the final victory that will give the earth back to you who created it. Then all will see and all will understand; humankind will be one, and all people will acknowledge your might and accept your love. In happy anticipation that day is mine already, Lord.

All the ends of the earth have seen the saving power of our God.

Psalm 99

Holy, Holy, Holy

I begin my prayer on my knees; I bow to the ground; I close my eyes and worship in silence the majesty of your infinite presence. Holiness is your name, Lord, and my lips are polluted with the dust of lies and the breath of conceit. I want to express with my prostration and my silence the feeling of total adoration that fills me when I appear before your holy presence. Accept the humble homage of my heart, O Lord.

I often deal with you in familiarity and friendship, and I treasure those moments and value that closeness. But I am conscious all the time that I belong down here in the dirt of the earth while your place is in heaven. I know the distance, and that is why I appreciate all the more your coming close and dealing with me as a friend. I take full advantage of your offer, and my whole life is full of those intimate dialogues with you in freedom and confidence, daily witness to your generous condescension.

But today I want to revert to my stand as a creature and offer you my silent worship in reverence on bended knee.

Let us extol Yahweh, our God. Holy is God!

You are holy with a holiness that is above all my concepts and beyond all my experience. The purity of a mountain spring, the flight of a bird in the sky, the path of the clouds, the silent falling of immaculate snow. These are images in my mind for portraying the remoteness of your essence in the limits of my experience. Others are the flame of fire, the sheet of lightning, the eye of the storm, the center of the earthquake—all that is great and awesome and pristine and pure. I ask for the sense of your holiness to pervade my whole being; I ask to be touched with a spark of your fire and a tremor of your storm. I want to learn reverence in my dealings with you, to temper the promptness of my feelings with the dignity of my respect. I want to be trained in the good manners of the heavenly court so as to practice heaven while still here on earth. I want to be your worshipper, Lord, as I am your companion and your friend. And I invite all those who know you to do the same.

Extol Yahweh, our God; worship at God's holy mountain, for holy is Yahweh, our God!

Psalm 100

The Sheep of His Flock

I am yours, Lord, in so far as I am a member of your flock. Give me that sense of belonging to your people on earth and, through your people, to you. I am no isolated individual; I have no claim to personal attention; I am not saved alone. It is true that you, Lord, love me for my own sake and look after my welfare and direct my steps, but you have chosen to work among humankind through the groups you have formed, through the people you have shaped. You deal with us as a shepherd with his flock. He does pay attention to every sheep and tends with special care the one that needs it most at any moment, but he leads them together and grazes them together and shelters them together in the unity of the flock.

Make me feel a member of the flock, Lord. Make me feel responsible, sociable, amiable, kin to my brothers and my sisters, and accountable to all human beings. Never for a moment allow me to think that I can go it alone, that I don't need anybody, that the lives of others do not concern me. Don't let me isolate myself in haughty pride or fallacious self-sufficiency. Don't let me be a loner. Don't let me be a stranger in my own land.

Make me feel proud of my brothers and sisters, appreciate their qualities and love their company. Make me feel at home in the flock, sense its support, and value the strength that being together brings to the group and to me in it. Make me contribute to the life of the others and allow them to contribute to mine. Make me enjoy going out together into common pastures, playing together, working together, living our life together. Make me be a community person in the full and blessed sense of the term. Make me do well in the group, that, seeing myself appreciated, I may also appreciate the others and contribute to the common unity.

I am a member of the flock because you are the Shepherd. You are the source of unity, and our dependence on you makes us happily seek our safety in you and thus meet each other under the shadow of your staff. Let my loyalty to you make me be loyal, too, to all the members of the flock. Let me trust others because I trust you. Make me love all because I love you. And may all people under your care learn to stand together for your sake.

Know that Yahweh is God! Yahweh made us, and we belong to God; we are God's people and the sheep of God's pasture.

Psalm 101

Resolutions

Today I bring before you, Lord, the list of my resolutions. It is now the end of a retreat, the beginning of a new year, or just a day of awakening in which I have looked at myself and at my life, and I have jotted down a few points to remind myself, and I ask you to bless them now. Here they are.

I will walk in the way of integrity. . . . In my household I will walk with a blameless heart. I will not let my eyes rest on any evil deed. I hate those who act perversely; they shall be far from me. Crooked hearts must keep their distance; I avoid the wicked. Those who secretly slander their neighbor I will silence. . . . I look to those who are faithful to dwell in my household.

I know I could have been more concrete, and in practice I'll do it if you so desire, but for today I wanted to set myself guidelines that will focus my efforts and direct my day. I want to strive for purity and wisdom in my actions; I will watch my thoughts from which actions follow; I will stop backbiting; and I will prize loyalty. Bless my resolutions in your house, O Lord.

I know only too well that resolutions by themselves achieve nothing. I could show you whole lists that I have made, year after year, with the sincerity of the fervent moment and the overconfidence of immature youth, lists that are only repeated records of naive good will and utter failure, carefully written lists with measured handwriting and numbered entries in order of importance. Written only to be forgotten. Recorded only to be filed away. My resolutions count for nothing, and experience has taught me that lesson with inescapable clarity.

That is why today I have just told you my thoughts; I have outlined before you the paths I would like my behavior to follow. Today that list is not a record but a prayer; that is, it is a list for you, not for me. It is for you to remember, to keep in mind, and to enact. They are not successes for me to achieve but graces for you to grant. They are not to be achieved by my effort but your power. Or rather they are to be achieved by you and me together, working hand in hand for the good of my soul and the welfare of your household.

My song is about faithfulness and justice; Yahweh, I sing it to you.

Psalm 102

I Love My City

I love your very stones and the dust of your streets. You are my city, my Zion, my heavenly Jerusalem; you, you are the city where I live, whose streets I walk, whose corners I know, whose air I breathe, whose buildings I love. You, you are the city given to me to be my home, my place on earth, my shelter in life, my urban link with humankind. You are figure and sign of the City of God. I love you; I am proud of you; I am happy to live in you, to show you to visitors, to give your name next to mine in my address, linking my name with yours in the topographical bond of residential marriage. You are my city, and I rejoice in you.

I love you as you are, dust and all. I could worship the stones in your streets and take them as altars to offer on them a sacrifice of praise. Your lanes are sacred, your crossroads are blessed, your houses are anointed with the presence of human beings, the children of God. You are a temple, the whole of you, consecrating the virgin landscapes of planet earth with the seal of working human beings.

I pray for you, for your beauty, and for your glory, to that God whose temple you are and whose majesty you reflect, that he may repair the wounds inflicted on you by the thoughtlessness of humankind and the ravages of time and that he may make you shine with the final perfection I dream for you, and he, as your Lord and King, wants for you.

But you, Yahweh, endure forever; every age remembers you! Rise! Forgive Zion! Pity Zion, for it is time—at last the hour has come. Your servants love even Zion's stones and are moved to pity by the city's dust. Then the nations will revere your name, Yahweh, and all the rulers on earth will respect your glory when you found Zion anew and then appear in glory.

Your wounds are my wounds, and your trials are my trials. In praying for you I pray for me, derelict as I feel at times before failures and sickness and death. My hope for your restoration is my hope for my own immortality. I hang on to your walls and take courage in the firmness of your structures. My own life sometimes seems to crumble, and then I lean on you, hide in you, identify with you. When I suffer, I remember your sufferings, and when the shadows of my life lengthen I think of the shadows over your ruins. Then I also think of your foundations, firm and lasting from time immemorial, and I find faith for myself in the permanence of your history.

Modern city of strikes and protests, of bombs that explode, and of police sirens that wail in the night. I suffer with you and live with you in the hope that our suffering will bring redemption and I will be able to sing in you the praises of the Lord who made you and made me.

The children of your servants will have a home, and their descendants will dwell in your presence forever to praise your name in Jerusalem.

Psalm 103

Trust in God's Mercy

Bless Yahweh, O my soul, and remember God's faithfulness: in forgiving all your offenses, in healing all your diseases.

I want to sing your mercy, Lord, which I have experienced in my body and in my soul. You have forgiven my sins, and you have healed my sickness. You have defeated evil in me, evil that showed itself as rebellion in my soul and corruption in my body. One leads to the other. I am one whole and united being, and the whole of me, body and soul, reacts to my choices and my actions in blessing or in darkness as I stumble along the way of life.

It is over that whole of me that you have extended your healing hand, Lord, in a gesture of pardon and of grace that restores my life and quickens my body. My very bones rejoice as I feel the blessing of your mercy in the depths of my being. Thank you, Lord, for your infinite goodness.

As the height of heaven over earth is the greatness of Yahweh's faithful love for those who fear God. Yahweh takes our sins away farther than the east is from the west. As tenderly as parents treat their children, so Yahweh has compassion on those who fear God. Yahweh knows what we are made of; Yahweh remembers that we are dust.

You know my weakness, because you made me. I have failed numberless times, and I know I shall fail again. My body will reflect the failings of my soul in the breaking down of its functions. I expect your mercy to come on me again, Lord, as it has done now and will always do, because you never fail those who love you. Heal my body and my soul to renew my life once more.

Bless Yahweh, O my soul, . . . in redeeming your life from destruction, in crowning you with love and compassion, in filling your years with good things, in renewing your youth like an eagle's.

Like an eagle's flight is my life on the horizons of your grace. Strong and firm, high and majestic. I feel my youth renewed and my strength affirmed. The whole sky is mine, because it is yours, and you now give it to me in my night. My youth surges through my veins as I survey the world with peaceful joy and gentle pride. How great are you, Lord, who have created all this and me with it! I bless you forever in the gratefulness of my soul.

Bless Yahweh, O my soul.

Psalm 104

Harmony in Creation

I want to discover the beauty of your creation, Lord, by thinking of the hand that made it. You are behind each star and each blade of grass, and the unity of your power gives unity and light to all that you created.

You spread the heavens out like a tent; you build your high walls upon the waters above. The clouds are your chariot as you travel on the wings of the wind.

It is your presence that gives strength to the mountains and speed to the rivers; you give the ocean its depth and the sky its color. You shepherd the clouds through the heavens and send down the timely gift of rain. You lead the birds in their flight and help the stork build its nest. You give the ox its strength and the gazelle its grace. You let the sea monsters play in the ocean and let fish without number teem in its depths.

You care for all of them; you watch over their lives; you direct their paths, and you give them food for strength and for joy.

All creatures depend on you to give them food in due season. You give the food they eat; with generous hand, you fill them with good things.

And humankind is in the midst of it all—to see your work, to enjoy its blessings, and to thank you for them. How much more will you care for them, heirs of your earth and rulers of creation! You feed them with the fruits of the earth to build their bodies and free their minds.

You bring forth food out from the earth: wine to make them rejoice, oil to make them happy, and bread to make them strong.

And to watch over them you send the moon and the stars; you order the days and the seasons for the rhythms of their lives;

you light their universe with the sun and cover their sleep with darkness.

You made the moon to mark the seasons; the sun knows the hour of its setting. You form the shadows, night falls, and all the forest animals prowl about. . . . At sunrise they retire, to lie down in their lairs. People go out to work and to labor until the evening.

Everything is in order; everything is in harmony. Countless creatures live together, and they greet one another with the variety of their faces and the swiftness of their paths. Each one enhances the beauty of the other, and all together form the eternal marvel that is our universe.

There is only one discordant note in the concert of creation. That is sin. It is there as a blot on the landscape, as a cleft in the earth, as a rift in the sky. It disturbs the balance of the human world; it blackens human history and endangers the human future. Sin is the one thing out of place in the universe and out of place in the human heart. When I look at creation I feel that violent trait that disfigures the work of the Creator, and my contemplation of the disturbed universe ends, as the psalm ends, with the poignant cry from my wounded heart:

May sinners vanish from the earth, and the wicked exist no more!

Psalm 105

Don't Touch My Servants!

Few words from your lips have moved me more, Lord, than this declaration in your psalm:

"Do not touch my anointed, . . . do not harm my prophets!"

Lord, I am unworthy, but I am your servant. I represent you; I speak in your name. And you are warning the rulers of the earth along my way not to touch me, because your hand is upon me. Thank you, Lord. Thank you for your love, for your care, for your protection. Thank you for engaging your word and your power in my cause, for standing by me, for fighting by my side. Thank you for your readiness to punish people who do me harm. You have come into the open to show me favor, and I treasure your words and your gesture, Lord.

I had set about singing once more the history of the salvation of your people (and me with them) through desert and sea, out of bondage into the promise, and I see it now summed up in that decisive admonition: "Don't touch my servants!" It resounds from Pharaoh's palace to the sides of the Jordan; it opens up ways and wins battles; it restrains enemies and defeats armies. It marks the pilgrimage of the people of God day by day with the power of faith and the confidence of victory. It is itself the whole history of the chosen people. "Don't touch my people." And the people reaches the Promised Land.

Those words explain my own history too, Lord, and I see that now. How am I where I am? How have I reached here? How do I find myself in the safety of your Church and the blessing of your grace? How is it the world has not overcome me, temptation has not overpowered me? Because one day early in my life you pronounced the royal warning: "Don't touch him; he is my servant." Your word protected me. Your warning defended me. Your promise guided me. I am what I am today because your words have gone ahead of me clearing the way and removing the dangers. Your words are my history. They are consoling words that built your people and shaped my life. Words that give firmness of heart and confidence in trouble because they come from you and declare the seriousness of your intent. I love to hear and to repeat those words: promise, covenant, oath, decree. I rejoice to see them piled up in the verses of your psalm:

God remembers the covenant forever: the promise for a thousand generations, the pact made with Abraham and Sarah, the oath to Isaac and Rebekah. Yahweh established it by decree as an everlasting covenant for Israel.

All those beautiful words are summed up in that practical command from your lips: "Don't touch my people"! That is your promise and your oath, the way to carry out your covenant and your decree. Your people will be protected, and your word will be fulfilled. Those few decisive words will write the whole glorious history of your pilgrim people.

When they were easily counted, few in number, strangers to the country, they went from nation to nation, from one kingdom to another people. God let no one oppress them and rebuked rulers on their behalf. "Do not touch my anointed," God said; "do not harm my prophets!"

I take in the full import of your words: "Don't touch my servants, because whoever touches them touches me!" Isn't that what you mean, Lord? And isn't that enough to move my heart and open my chest in gratitude and love? You take as done to you what is done to me. You identify with me. You make me one with you. I don't deserve the grace, but I fathom the privilege. I am grateful for the safety this word brings to me, but I am much more grateful for the practical assurance of love and care from you that it effects and signifies.

"Do not touch my anointed, . . . do not harm my prophets!"

Thank you, Lord, in the name of your prophets and your servants.

Psalm 106

Israel's Short Memory

That was the trouble with Israel, source and cause of all its troubles: it had a short memory. The people of Israel saw the greatest wonders a people has ever seen and experienced in its history. But they clean forgot. No sooner had they seen the miracle than they forgot about it. They experienced God's protection in wonderful ways, but soon it was with them as though nothing had happened, and they fell to fearing new dangers and to displeasing the Lord who so faithfully had helped them, and they doubted that he could do it again. And so they suffered and they provoked God's anger. That was the great weakness of Israel as a people: it had a short memory.

Our ancestors, when they were in Egypt, gave no thought to your wonderful works; they did not remember the abundance of your steadfast love. God did wonders for them, yet *they forgot God, their Savior, who had done great things in Egypt.*

I, too, have a short memory, Lord. I just forget. I don't recall what you have done for me. Your wonderful acts of mercy and power for me in my life are just not present in my memory when I come to face the dangers of a new day. And I fear and suffer, and, what is worse, I irritate you who have done so much for me and are ready to do it again. If only I would let you act by looking at you with gratitude and confidence.

I forget. I tremble in the face of difficulties I have surmounted before, I cower before sufferings I have formerly endured with your grace. I feel diffident when your grace has shown me a hundred times that I will be successful; I run away from battles much less formidable than others you have made me win before.

It is not that I don't know my past. I recall its events, and I can write down my own history. I know, yes, the moments when

202

you have intervened in my life in a special way to give it a new turn upwards, to save it from dangers, to lead it into glory. I know all that, to be sure, but I forget its significance, its importance, its message. I forget that every act of yours is not only an action but a message; it not only gives help now but promises deliverance forever; it not only does, it signifies. And it is that significance, that reassurance, and that promise that I miss and I forget.

Teach me, Lord, to understand; teach me to remember. Teach me to give to each of your actions in my life the value it has as a concrete assistance and as a permanent sign. Teach me to read into your actions the message of your love, that I may never forget and never doubt that you will always be with me in the future as you have been in the past.

Then they believed God's promises; they sang praise. With them I, too, will sing your praises, Lord. *Let all the people say, "Amen!"*

Book V

Psalm 107

The Dangers of Life

Danger and deliverance. That is the routine of life. It was so in antiquity, and it is so with us. The dangers may vary in shape or in name, but the fear when they come is the same, and the relief when they go is the same, as the same is the hand of the Lord that delivers us from them.

The ancient people list four dangers: desert, prison, sickness, and storm at sea. And four deliverances: from the hunger and thirst of the desert to the straight road to a fortified city, from the darkness of the hidden dungeon to the light of freedom, from sickness to health, and from the stormy sea to the safety of the harbor.

In my life too, Lord, there is the dryness of the desert, the darkness of the dungeon, the weakness of the body, and the uncertainty of sea and air and even land under threats of war and attacks of terrorists near home. Humankind has not improved in two thousand years. Human life is very much the same today in the traffic of the city as it was in the sands of the desert. I live with danger; I fear calamities; I fall prey to suffering; I collapse in despair.

I, too, need the hand that delivers me from the dangers in my life. From my desert and my dungeon and my storm. I need your hand, Lord; I need your guidance and your light; I need your power and your strength. I need again and again in my day-to-day life the nearness of your presence and the healing of your touch. I need deliverance because I am not free.

I pray for freedom from sickness, but more than that I pray for freedom from the fear of sickness. That is the deliverance I pray for. Not so much the deliverance from the outside danger as from the inward fear. So long as the deliverance does not come, I shall never be free, because the danger is always there. I want to be free from fears, and then the desert and the sea and all the prisons and wars of the world will have no effect on me.

Some had strayed in the wilderness and the desert, not finding a way to an inhabited town. Hungry and thirsty, their life was wasting away. Then they cried to Yahweh in their anguish, and Yahweh rescued them from their distress, guiding them by a straight road to a city where they could live. Let them thank Yahweh for this faithful love, for these deeds on our behalf. Satisfying the hungry, Yahweh fills the hungry with good things.

Give me a fearless heart, Lord, a heart that believes and trusts in you, and as a result fears nobody and is afraid of nothing. Bring the blessing of your deliverance down to the very depths of my soul to pluck out the roots of fear and sow the seeds of peace. Give me confidence in my heart that I may live with joy, Lord. Be close to me, Lord, so that the dangers of existence may turn into the bliss of living.

Psalm 108

The Wheel of Life

You may get the impression at times, Lord, that I repeat myself in my prayers to you. Permit me to say, in recognition of a common situation, that you also repeat yourself in your Word, Lord. And, in a way, that is as it should be; it is proper that both you and I repeat ourselves when dealing with life, because life itself is repetition. Life is a cycle, a wheel, a routine. Life is day after night and night after day with the inevitability of the laws of the heavens and of the moods in the human heart. Don't mind, then, my repetitions, Lord, as I don't mind yours.

What I ask when the same prayers come to my hands and the same verses to my lips, when the same situations occur in my life and the same thoughts cross my mind, is to live the old situation with a new heart, to say the repeated prayer with a new faith, to love the routine of life with the newness of an open mind ready to take every day as new and every dawn as a surprise.

This psalm is made up of parts of two other psalms pieced together. My life also is made up of patches of old experiences lived again and again in the repeated framework of my own limitation. Give me the grace, Lord, to take each experience again as a new event, to find fresh every time the bread I receive from your hands at the beginning of each new day.

It is love that makes repetition pleasurable. Give me love, Lord, that every prayer may turn to joy on my lips.

Psalm 109

The Weapon of the Poor

People do not understand curses because people do not understand the poor. The helpless who have nowhere to turn, who suffer without remittance at the whim of the rich and the powerful, who know in their bones that they are the victims of injustice and yet find no redress in the bitterness of their days and the agony of their lives. What are they to do?

They have no power of their own, no money, no influence, no way to exert pressure or show strength the way those of the world do to force their way and get what they want. The poor have no weapons to fight in a world in which everyone is armed to the teeth. They have only the weapon of the word. As a member of the People of God, their word, when they speak in self-defense, is God's word, because the defense of a member is the defense of the whole People. And so they release the weapon, they charge each word with the ugliest calamities they can think of, and they utter the curse that is warning and notice and threat that God will do what the curse expresses if the enemy does not stop the attack and withdraw. The curse is the "nuclear deterrent" in a society that believes in the power of words.

The word is effective. It does what it says. It cannot be called back. The blessing will be blessing and the curse will be curse once it has left the lips of the poor who alone have the right to utter it, and it will go and fly and wreak ruin on the head of the wicked who persecute the poor, restoring justice to a world where justice is not done. The curse is the weapon used in self-defense by those who have no weapons.

I feel helpless, too, before the reign of injustice in the world today, and with the right that my helplessness gives me I use wholeheartedly the weapon you, Lord, put in my hands as member of your People and as poor among the poor.

May all the violent people be brought to nothing, may all oppressors, exploiters, profiteers, extortionists, all moneylenders, black marketeers, hoarders, speculators, and givers and takers of bribes be subdued forever; may all abductors, kidnappers, hijackers, and terrorists fall victim to their own terror; may those who kill by the sword die by the sword; may all dictators of every sign cease to dictate any more, and may all those who plot evil for others see that evil done to themselves. May these words spread their wings, hit their target, stem injustice, and bring peace to the poor you love, Lord.

I will give thanks aloud to Yahweh and praise God in the assembly for standing at the right hand of the poor against those who would have sentenced them to death.

Psalm 110

A Priest Forever

This is my psalm, Lord, your blessing for me, your reminder of the day my hands were anointed with your oil so that I could bless all people in your name. Your promise, your election, your consecration. Your word itself engaged me in the most sacred pledge of eternal commitment:

Yahweh has sworn and will not retract: "You are a priest forever after the order of Melchizedek."

Since that day the very name "Melchizedek" sounds like welcome music to my ears. His mysterious appearance, his royal priesthood, his offer of bread and wine, and his blessing with authority Abraham, in whom all faithful were also blessed. From Abraham comes my sacred lineage, the bread and wine in my hands, and the right to bless with authority all people and all leaders of humankind. Family tree of long biblical roots.

My priesthood is as mysterious as Melchizedek's. I never fathom the depth of its meaning; I look at my hands and wonder how they can forgive sins, bless children, and bring heaven down to the altars of earth. The greatness of my calling even creates in me doubts of identity and crises of unworthiness. How can the smallness of my being carry the majesty of your presence? How can I prove true to the trust placed on me? How can I persevere in the face of dangers that threaten my state and undermine my convictions?

The answer is your word, your promise, your oath. You have sworn that you will not change your purpose. You will not change your mind. You will not dismiss me. You will not allow me to break the sacred bond. And I don't want you to allow me to do so. I want your oath to stand firm for you and me. I want the firmness of your word where I fear the fickleness of my heart. I trust in you,

Lord. I trust in your trust in me. Let me never prove unworthy of that trust.

Do not change your purpose for me, Lord. And don't allow me to change it either.

Let your sacred words accompany me with love every day of my life: *You are a priest forever.*

Psalm 111

Community Prayer

Alleluia! I will thank you, Yahweh, with all my heart in the meeting of the just and their assembly.

I do not pray alone, Lord. I pray with my brothers and sisters, I pray with my group, with the friends who in your name and with your grace live and work together for the coming of your Kingdom. I pray in the group and with the group; I make mine the prayers of each one, and I know that all make my prayers their own. This is not only multiplying the number of lips that praise your name but giving the prayer a new meaning, a new dimension, a new depth, because the group, though small in itself, represents your whole People, and thus the prayer we make together is the prayer of your People before you. You love your People and you like to see it pray together. And we, too, like to pray together before you.

The very fact that we are together in your presence is a prayer. Our silence speaks; our posture prays; our awareness of each other is mute intercession. And our words, even when they are ordinary words and common expressions, are charged with feeling and care because we recognize each other's accents and know each other's histories. A short phrase may carry a whole life, and a simple expression may reveal a deep heart, because we know the lips that have spoken and the background of that phrase. No word is lost in the intimacy of the group that knows why that word has been spoken today.

When our voices unite in a common prayer, that prayer, too, acquires a new urgency, as the harmony of dissonant voices emphasizes the universality of the need we lay open before you. When we pray, the whole world prays, because we know its needs and live its aspirations. Even the individual's prayer for a personal need becomes universal in the group, because it acquires the public resonance of all those we know to suffer the same evil and need the same blessing. There is no egoism in common prayer, because each concrete need, when pronounced in the group, becomes symbol and carrier of all such needs in us and in all people.

The prayer we enjoy most together is the prayer of praise. Psalms were meant to be sung and sung not in the exclusiveness of the soloist but in the roaring sound of a tumultuous choir. We like to praise you together in words that are all the richer on our lips because they have been spoken by thousands of lips, and each time they are enriched with the memory of a new blessing and the recognition of a new grace. The praise of your People is precious to you, Lord, who receive it, as it is precious to us who in the joy of our hearts and the music of our voices offer it to you. Accept our petitions, our thanks, our worship, and our praise. We know that is our function as a people, and we do it most willingly in the daily comradeship of our group.

I will thank you, Yahweh, with all my heart in the meeting of the just and their assembly.

Bless our group, Lord. We are few, but we work hard; we are different, but we struggle for unity; we even make others suffer at times, but our love is stronger than our envy, and our commitment to one another in you is stronger than our grievances. Bless us in the daily routine that brings us together hour by hour in moments of tension and of relaxation, in running around and in work, in consultations and in prayer. Bless our planning together, our efforts to support, as a group, whatever any one of us does. Bless our growth into unity through noble ideals and earthly realities. Make us truly a company of good people that our praise may be pleasing to you.

I will thank you, Yahweh, with all my heart in the meeting of the just and their assembly.

Psalm 112
Portrait of the Just

I recollect with reverent attention the traits that define the just in the sight of God: *Happy those who fear Yahweh and joyfully keep God's commandments! . . . Even in the darkness, light dawns for the upright, for the merciful, compassionate, and righteous. . . . Quick to be generous, they give to the poor; their righteousness stands firm forever.*

The quest for perfection need not be complicated. Sanctity is within reach, and righteousness can be found at home. Joy to keep the law and compassion to help the poor are also close at hand. Common sense holds its own even in the spiritual life, and the simplicity of a true heart will find the shortcuts to holiness. The heart knows the way to be a good person, to be just, to be righteous, and to follow it is the elementary wisdom of all spiritual progress.

Sometimes I feel that we make the spiritual life too complicated. When I think of the many spiritual books I have read, the many courses I have followed, the many systems I have tried, the many practices I have adopted, I cannot help smiling good-naturedly to myself and asking myself whether I need to pass so many examinations in order to learn how to pray. And the answer I give myself is that all those religious studies are very fine in themselves, but they may well become a hindrance when I bend my knee and want to pray. It is easier than that to be just. I don't need the latest book on the spirituality market in order to find God in my life. So far I am finding only books. I want to go back to simplicity of mind and humility of spirit. Back to loving God and loving my neighbor, back to opening my mouth and reciting prayers I learned as a child, back to fearing the Lord and keeping his commandments with joy, back to being a kind and simple person in the midst of a sophisticated world, back to being what God called simply and directly "a just person."

Many are the blessings God piles up on the head of the just: *Children of such as these will be powers on earth; each generation of the upright will be blessed. There will be riches and wealth for their families, and their righteousness stands firm forever. . . . They are always stead-fast and leave an everlasting memory behind them. With a trusting heart and confidence in Yahweh, they need never fear evil news.*

Again, straightforward blessings for the straightforward person. Happiness in the home and security in life. The blessings of the earth as anticipation of the blessings of heaven. The just know that God's hand is on them in this life and that he will simply and humbly let it be happily there for all eternity. This is the ripe fruit in heaven of his goodness on earth.

Happy those who fear Yahweh!

Psalm 113

Strength in Weakness

I know something of your ways of acting with the children of humankind, Lord, and one of the norms you secretly follow and openly proclaim is that your strength is manifested in weakness. When human beings lift their heads in pride, they will be humbled; but when they recognize their own weakness, own it, and accept it, you fill the empty vessel of their acknowledged humility with the fullness of your power. Human weakness is God's strength. It has always been so.

You raise the poor from the dust and lift the needy from the dunghill to give them a place with rulers, with the nobles of your people. Yahweh, you give the barren a home, making them glad with children.

God brings fertility out of sterility and crowns the poor as rulers of his people. That is the Kingdom. Human values are upset, and earthly calculations discounted. The wisdom of the wise is confounded, and the cleverness of the clever is destroyed. The glory of God shines in the lowliness of humankind.

I want to experience your power, Lord. I want to feel the power of your Spirit when I speak in your name and when I act for your cause. And I am grateful to you for showing me now the way to release your power in my actions. I have to disappear that you may appear, I have to be dust that you may be light, I have to humble myself that you may do your work. So long as I am full of my own importance I am just obstructing the way for your power. The day I am nothing you will be everything. I must diminish that you may increase, as someone said while preparing the way for you. That is the law of prophets and apostles, of preachers of your word and workers of the Kingdom. Let me glory in my weakness that the fullness of your power may work through me.

Who is like you, Yahweh our God? Enthroned so high, you have to stoop to see the heavens and earth!

Psalms 114 & 115
Idols on My Altar

There is a verse in this psalm that haunts me, Lord, and you will understand me if I put aside in my consideration all the many other beautiful verses in this psalm, or rather in the two psalms united to make up this psalm, and I fix the eye of my faith and the hopes for my spiritual growth on that single verse that you utter here and repeat again word for word in a later psalm. It sounds like a proverb coming from your mouth, a principle of wisdom, a biblical curse of long consequences for a People in search of a Promised Land and for a heart in search of God. The proverb is: "Those who make idols will become like them."

I feel a chill run down my spine when I hear those words. I know that idols are wood and stone, and so to wood and stone are condemned those who make them. There are idol-makers in the outward sense of the word, craftspeople who fashion the images of the divinity as ordered by the variegated imagination of fanciful worshippers in all cultures and ages. Against them goes the direct invective of the psalm to enforce the Lord's commandment to his People not to make images of the divinity for themselves and also the invective to deride the ridiculous efforts of misguided piety in lifeless figures.

Their idols are silver and gold, the work of human hands. They have mouths but cannot speak; they have eyes but cannot see; they have ears but cannot hear; they have nostrils but cannot smell. With their hands they cannot feel; with their feet they cannot walk. No sound comes from their throats. Those who make them will be like them and so will all who trust in them.

And then there are idol-makers in a more subtle sense of the term, all the more dangerous for being less obvious, and it is there that I see myself and feel on my head the weight of the biblical indictment. I make idols in my mind, and I worship them with hidden fidelity and stubborn submission. Idols are my prejudices, my judgments, my tastes and distastes, my own ideas of how things should be, my values and principles however legitimate they may appear to me, my habits and customs, my own past experiences that now rule my present life, and whatever I have assumed, taken for granted, fixed in my mind and made into an inflexible rule of conduct for myself and for all people forever.

All those are idols—idols of the mind. They may be wood and stone, or even gold and silver, but in any case they are dead metal unworthy of a living soul. They can be mental idols, ideological idols, cultural idols, or even spiritual idols—all the dead weight of a long life, all the unhappy baggage of the past. They are burden and bondage, slavery and chains, sorry heritage of my heathen spirit.

What frightens me now is the penalty attached to the worship of idols: to be like them. To have eyes that do not see, to have ears that do not hear, to have hands that do not feel, and to have feet that do not walk. To lose my sense, my contact with reality, my life. That is the punishment for sticking to an idol in my mind: to cease to be alive. I worship my old ideas; I hold on to my prejudices; I hang on to the past, and I lose the capacity to see the present. I clog my memory with custom and routine and cease to see and hear and sense and walk. I become wood and stone. I become dead. I have worshipped my past in search of security and comfort, and I find the black night of insensitivity and death. The idol is a fixed notion, and when I hold on to a fixed notion I become fixed like it in wood and stone.

You hated idols, Lord, throughout your recorded utterances to your chosen People. I ask you today to free me from all idols in my life, that I may walk again.

Psalm 116a

Passion and Resurrection

This psalm was prayed on the way to Gethsemane. Supper was over, the group was small, the final thanksgiving hymn, the Hallel, had to be recited, and they did so as they crossed the valley on the way to a garden with old olive trees where some rested, some slept, and under the full moon shadow a frail figure fell on his face in prayer to his Father for delivery from death. His words were an echo of one of the psalms of the Hallel he had just recited. The psalm, through its yearly recitation at the Paschal meal and this day through its timely recollection on the way to death, was the final acceptance of the Father's will by him whose purpose in coming to earth was to do that will.

The cords of death encompassed me; the pangs of Sheol laid hold on me; I suffered sorrow and anguish. Then I called on your name, Yahweh: "Oh Yahweh, I beseech you, save my life!"

I approach this psalm with inward reverence knowing that lips holier than mine have prayed it in the face of death. But despite the infinite distances I, too, have a right to say it, because I, too, in my human misery know the despair of life and the terror of death. The seal of death marks me from the moment of my birth, not only in the mortality of my body but also in the existential anguish of my soul. I know myself on my way to the tomb, and the shadow of that day falls on all the other days of my life. And when that final day approaches, everything within me revolts and protests and clamors for a postponement of the inevitable hour. I am mortal, and I bear the brunt of my mortal condition in the very essence of my being.

But then I also know that the loving Father who brought me to birth awaits me just as lovingly after death. I know that life continues, that my real existence will begin only then on the other side of eternity. I accept the fact that as I am mortal so I am also eternal, and life will be mine forever in the final glory of my Father's house.

I have faith in life after death, and I take heart with the thought that the words of the psalm that bring me comfort today also brought comfort on a bleak Thursday night to another troubled soul who said them in the solitude of a garden before the dawn of his last day on earth:

I will walk before you, Yahweh, in the land of the living.

Psalm 116b

Renewal of Vows

I will fulfill what I vowed to you in the presence of all the people.

I am happy, Lord, that I took my vows. I am happy about the day in my youth when, with open generosity and blissful enthusiasm, I publicly consecrated my life to you in poverty, chastity, and obedience. I am proud of that moment and look back on it as a new birth in your service and in the service of humankind for your sake. I am glad I took my vows and want to renew them today, in thanksgiving for that day and in the clear determination that if I had not taken them then I would take them now. Accept again the consecration of my life, Lord, as you accepted it that day, and keep in me the joy this consecration has given me.

I know now more about poverty, chastity, and obedience than on the first day I pronounced those three words aloud and together in the presence of my brothers and on my knees before your altar. I have measured with my own failings the depth of my commitment, and I have learned with my mistakes the practical meaning of the lofty ideal.

Even today I have doubts at times; I am questioned by others, and I don't know how to answer; I hear about new interpretations and more meaningful approaches, and sometimes I fail to recognize my original notions under the new vocabulary. But I know well what I mean, what those three sacred words mean in my life and in my history, as in the history and tradition of the People of God whose lot and representative and servant I am. I am committed to you, Lord, mind, body, and soul, for the glory of your name and for the service of all people; that is the strong and clear conviction of my heart. Now I ask for your grace to make that conviction my daily conduct and to translate my verbal commitment into actual practice.

That conviction is the meaning of my renewal of vows. This renewal of vows is not only a yearly custom but a daily privilege. I like to pronounce those three words again together, in the silence of my soul before you, and in the company of my brothers when we all renew our bonds by pledging our lives. And with those words goes a prayer that the spirit those vows represent may become stronger and stronger in my life and in the group, that my commitment and my service may grow into wisdom and joy as my years increase and my initial consecration takes on new meanings without my ever forgetting the old.

I will fulfill what I vowed to you in the presence of all the people in the courts of the house of Yahweh, in your midst, Jerusalem.

Psalm 117

A Short Prayer

Prayers need not be long, and if I truly feel what I pray, the intensity of the feeling more than makes up for the length and the time of the recitation.

I put in my prayer a word of divine praise, the consciousness of the group, and the universality of humankind, my faith in God's love and his faithfulness to his promise of salvation, and a perfect prayer is made.

Alleluia! Praise Yahweh, all you nations; glorify Yahweh, all you peoples, for God's love is strong, God's faithfulness eternal.

Psalm 118

The Joy of Easter

These are sounds of Easter Sunday: shouts of victory over death and confidence in the Lord's power, rejoicing in the common triumph, and proclaiming this the day of days over any other day that the Lord has made.

With Yahweh on my side, best help of all, I can triumph over my enemies. . . . I am not abandoned to death. Open the gates of justice to me. . . . The stone rejected by the builders has become the cornerstone; this is Yahweh's doing, and it is marvelous to see. This is the day made memorable by Yahweh. Let us rejoice and be glad.

This is the liturgy of Easter in the memory of the Christian. But then, for the true Christian every Sunday is Easter, and every day is Sunday. Thus every day is Easter, every day is *the day made memorable by Yahweh*, the day on which the Lord has acted. Every day is a day of victory and praise, of rejoicing and thanksgiving, a day of practicing the final resurrection by conquering sin, which is death, and breathing joy, which is eternity.

"This is the day on which the Lord has acted." How I wish I could say that of every day in my life! I know it is true, because if I am alive it is because God is acting in me with his infinite power and merciful grace. But I want to feel God's presence, to sense it, to see it in faith and experience, recognizing God's hand in the turns of my day and feeling his breath as I move in the human world. This is his day, glorious as Easter and mighty as the dawn of creation, and I want the eyes of faith to see the figure of his glory in the humility of my goings and comings.

Yahweh's right hand is lifted high. Yahweh's right hand has done mighty things. I shall not die, but live to proclaim the deeds of Yahweh.

Let the truth of my faith sink into my mind and flower in my actions: a Christian is a person who lives the spirit of Easter—the spirit of struggle and victory, of faith and perseverance, of joy after suffering and life after death. No calamity will crush me; no temporary defeat will discourage me. I live already in the day of days, and I know that the hand of the Lord will always be victorious at the end. *With Yahweh at my side helping me, what can anyone do to me?*

By myself I cannot achieve the spirit of Easter in my life. As on Easter Sunday I stand in the midst of the congregation that proclaims its faith and strengthens mine by standing together and singing together the marvels of our God. So now, day by day, I also need the group around me to proclaim the same conviction and confirm my Easter faith with the gift of theirs. I invite the house of Israel, the house of Aaron, and all those who fear the Lord to sing with me the glory of Easter, that we all may grow into its spirit together.

I give thanks to you Yahweh, for you are good; your love is everlasting! Let the house of Israel say, "Your love is everlasting!" . . . Let those who fear Yahweh say, "Your love is everlasting!"

Psalms 119

Prayer of the Young

How shall people be pure in their ways? By keeping to your words.
Your word. This is a long meditation—since young people are generous with their lives and with their time—on your Law. To bring out its different aspects, different words are used for it in the drawn-out study: Laws, statutes, commands, ordinances, decrees, precepts, promises, words. They are woven together in acrostic stanzas along the letters of the Hebrew alphabet with the loving repetition of a young scholar who wants to master the mystery and the practice of the divine Law.

Blessed are you, Yahweh. Teach me your statutes. With my lips I recited all the ordinances of your mouth. I rejoice in the way of your decrees with joy above all wealth. I will meditate on your precepts and concentrate on your ways. I will delight in your statutes and never forget your words.

Your divine will, Lord, is the law of my life. I want to know it, to accept it, to practice it day by day and hour by hour. I want to understand the depth of your designs and rejoice in the execution of your desires.

How I love your law, O God! I think of it all the day.

And all life long. The study that never ends because your law is your will, and your will is yourself, divine essence and infinite being. The study that is contemplation and worship in faith and in love. The study that brings wisdom and joy to the young people who make it the love of their youth.

I understand more than all my teachers when your law is my meditation. I have more discernment that the elders because I observe your precepts.

Teach me, Lord, to see your will in the laws of nature and in the accidents of life, in the regulations that govern peoples and in the events that befall humankind, in the orders from authority and in the promptings of my heart. Your will is all that happens, because you are in all things and your dominion is supreme. To see you in all things and your will in all events is the way to wisdom and happiness and peace. Let me learn that one lesson in the leisurely meditation of the depths of your law.

Let my cry come before you, O God; in keeping your word, give me understanding. May my supplication reach you; deliver me according to your promise. My lips pour forth your praise because you teach me your statutes. My tongue sings of your promise, for all your commandments are just. . . . Your law is my delight.

Let your Law be truly my delight, Lord.

Psalm 120

The Exile's Prayer

You liars, what will God do to you? . . . Living among you is as bad as living in Meshech, or among the people of Kedar!

Strange names, Meshech and Kedar. Strange lands for those who love their homes and are forced to dwell in far-off places with people they do not know and a language they do not understand. The curse of modern humankind. The sin of our civilization. The exile, the expatriate, the refugee. Whole groups of people uprooted from their land, or single individuals persecuted for their beliefs. Human beings have to flee from other human beings, have to hide their faces from their brothers and sisters. Scars of fear on the face of humankind.

I pray for all those who have been deprived of their right to live in their land, who have been forcibly ejected, discriminated against, persecuted, expelled. I pray for all those who have had to build a new home away from their true home and live in a culture alien to their own culture, for all those who come from one country while their children are born in another, who bear the strain of uniting two traditions in one home; and for all those who dream of a promised land while camping in the desert. I pray for all the exiles on earth that they may preserve their roots while growing new flowers, that they may find friendship and give love, that their neighbors may become their brothers and sisters, and that their wanderings may remind humankind that we all are one. I pray that their exile may strengthen their personality and confirm their values while they learn to appreciate the new values around them and assimilate them into their own. I pray that they may feel as exiles no longer, but may make themselves at home in mind and in body and prosper where they are with the warmth of their hope and the strength of their faith.

As I pray for them I realize I am praying for me, too. I, too, am an exile. I, too, live in Meshech and Kedar, away from home among people who do not speak my language. The language of the spirit is an unknown language over here. The society where I live speaks the language of money, success, power, or violence. I don't understand that language, and I feel lost in my own world. I long for other landscapes and other fields. I know I am on my way, and I feel the anxiety of the exile and the impatience of the pilgrim.

I want for me now the synthesis I have desired for others. I want to keep my roots and give new flowers; to treasure my own culture while I assimilate those of others; to love my home and love my exile too, showing in my active resignation the hope that can convert the desert into a garden and earth into heaven.

I am an exile today in order to be a citizen of heaven forever.

Psalm 121

My Weak Points

Yahweh guards you, shades you. With Yahweh at your right hand the sun cannot harm you by day nor the moon at night.

I know the meaning, Lord, of that image of ancient warfare. I stand with the sword or the spear in my right hand, ready to strike, while my left hand holds the protecting shield over my body. That shield covers the front and left side of my body but leaves my right side uncovered when I throw the spear or wield the sword. You, my guardian, know that, and that is why you stand at my right hand, to protect with your shield what I leave unprotected with mine, my vulnerable side at that moment, the weak point in my defense. Thank you, Lord, for your knowledge of the dangers of the world, your knowledge of my own weakness, and your readiness to protect me where I need it most.

I have my weaknesses, Lord, and it is a comfort to me to realize that you know them better than I myself know them. I am well-meaning and faithful, but I have moods and tempers and passions and fits, and I never know what I may do before a sudden opposition or an unexpected test. My right side is naked, and any flying arrow may find its deadly way into my open body. Stand at my right hand and cover me, Lord.

Make me aware of my weak points, of my blind spots, of my hidden dangers. Open my eyes to those flaws in me that all my friends know so well and that I alone seem to be unaware of. Make me see what everybody sees in me, what so often annoys them without my realizing it, what they discuss about me among themselves without ever telling me. Make me notice my most common failings, remember them, and protect for the future those sides of my personality that I see weak and undefended. Keep your guard over me, Lord, as there will always be something left exposed, and I will need your shield to cover me in moments of danger.

Yahweh guards you from harm, protects your lives; Yahweh watches over your coming and going, now and for always.

Psalm 122

City of Peace

Jerusalem, your name is peace, yet you have never seen peace since your foundation. You are meant to be a city where people come together in unity, and yet throughout history they have come to you to fight. Your walls were built and demolished, a new Temple was erected on the ruins of the old; you have seen many rulers sit on David's throne, and today armed police patrol your narrow streets day and night.

Jerusalem, what has become of your peace? Was it a sin to proclaim it? Was it a provocation to call yourself the City of Peace? Why is your history so torturing and your sky so darkened with hatred? Is your name City of Peace or City of Fear? Are you not the heart of all the tribes of Israel, the cradle of believing humankind, the home of all the children of God? Why are you news in the papers instead of blessing in a prayer? Why have you to be protected, you whose aim and duty was to protect all people who came to you?

I always consider myself as on my way to you. Perpetual pilgrim of your eternal charm. Always dreaming of your gates, walking towards your temple, scanning the horizon for the profile of your towers against the sky. For me your name means everything I have to reach in this life and in the next. Justice, holiness, salvation, peace. You are symbol and hope, fantasy and prayer, poetry and stone. I am always walking toward you, and my heart rejoices when it exhorts my brothers and sisters: "Let us go to the house of the Lord!"

I wish you well, Jerusalem! May your markets prosper and your gardens flower; may your people come together and your towers stand. And above all may you be true to your name, may you have peace and give it to all who come to you in search of it from all corners of the world.

Pray for peace in Jerusalem: "Security to your houses! Peace inside your city walls! Security to your towers!" Since all are my neighbors and friends, I say, "Peace be with you!" Since Yahweh our God lives here, I pray for your good.

Psalm 123

My Eyes' Prayer

My eyes speak as they turn, and so today my eyes are praying as they turn to you, Lord.

To you I have lifted up my eyes, you who dwell in the heavens.

My eyes are lifted up, as in figure and imagery you are in heaven, and heaven is on high. While I live the routine of my days my eyes are usually down to watch my own step, or looking ahead of me, not in order to see people but in order not to bump into them. I see people and traffic, then buildings and rooms, papers and books, flashing colors and printed words. I see a thousand images in a passing instant. Only I don't see you.

When I talk with people I am aware that my eyes speak too. They give me away. They express likes and dislikes, interest and boredom, instant pleasure or flashing anger. A twinkle of the eye can be more expressive than a whole speech. A loving regard can convey more affection than a love poem. My eyes speak silently, tenderly, effectively.

Today my eyes are turned to you, Lord. And that is prayer. No words, no petitions, no praises. Just my eyes turned to heaven. I know that you can read their message and understand their language. A tender look of faith and devotion, of confidence and love. Just looking at you. Gently turning my eyes up. I feel it does me good. My eyes tell me that they like to look up. I let them follow their liking, and I accompany the direction of their look with the longing of my soul.

Like the eyes of slaves are on the hand of their master, like the eyes of servants on the hand of their mistress, so our eyes are on you, Yahweh our God, till you show us your mercy.

Psalm 124

Deliverance

In my dark moments I think, Lord, that life is a trap. Forgive me for saying so before you who made life and are responsible for its working, but I sometimes feel I am just trapped in the mesh of a worthless and senseless existence like a bird in a fowler's snare. It is no use flapping my wings, no use straining my legs. I am trapped in the iron grip of my own mortal doubt. I can go nowhere. Maybe there is nowhere to go.

Of all the depressions that come over me this sense of helplessness is the most grievous one. I feel I can do nothing. I feel I am nothing. A lump of clay, an inert mass, an existential cipher. My life is of no account, if it can be called life at all. I mean nothing to anybody, least of all to myself. My coming into this world has made no difference to humankind, neither will my going from it. The wind comes and goes, but it at least sways the flowers and makes the trees sing. I count for nothing. I feel nothing. I see life as a cruel game in which I am tossed to and fro without ever being asked where I want to go and what I want to do. Or, truer still, the deadly fact is that I don't know where I want to go and what I want to do; it is in my own self that the roots of my helplessness are grounded. And that is my despair.

I am trapped, body and soul, in a trap of my own making. Maybe I expected too much from life, from myself, from you, Lord, if I may speak to you when even your existence means nothing to me (and allow me to say so before you, if only to manifest to you the extent of my dereliction). I had hopes that never materialized, and dreams that never came true. Life has played me false with the ruthless indifference of a cruel game. I am stuck in the misery of a meaningless birth.

My only prayer today, Lord, (and even that I have to borrow word for word from the psalm as I can frame no prayer on my own) is that you deliver me from my present darkness so that I may soon make mine, in my heart, the words you have inspired:

We have escaped like a bird from the hunter's trap; the trap has been broken and we are free! Our help comes from Yahweh, the Maker of heaven and earth.

Break my trap soon, Lord!

Psalm 125

Endurance

Those who trust in you, Yahweh, are like Mount Zion, which cannot be moved, but endures forever.

The sight of a mountain always brings joy to my heart. I guess the reason is that a mountain speaks of perseverance, solidity, and endurance, and I need those virtues in my life. A mountain on the horizon is what I would like to be, steadfast and firm. That is why I like to sit on the rocks and look steadily at the mountain in front of me: that long look is a prayer that the steadfastness of the mountains may come into my life.

"Mount Zion cannot be moved." I cannot say the same about myself. Any little wind of adversity shakes me to my foundations and pulls me to the ground. And, again, any breeze of empty flattery lifts me up above myself, only to dash me with greater violence on the rock of despair. I waver, I hesitate, I doubt. I lose courage and lack constancy. I begin many plans and I drop them half way. I promise regular practice, and I interrupt it at the first obstacle. I cannot trust myself. And now you, Lord, point out to me the road to constancy: to trust in you. *Those who trust in you . . . are like Mount Zion.* Trust in you is my support and my strength.

Teach me to trust you, Lord, that my life may be firm. Teach me to rely on you, since I cannot rely on myself. Teach me to climb Mount Zion in desire and in faith, in order to find in its summit what I lack in my valley. Teach me to lean on the eternal rock of your word, your promise, your love, that I may find in you what I have never been able to find in myself. Let me feel in my life the lovable words of your psalm:

As the mountains are round about Jerusalem, so you are round about your people both now and forevermore.

Psalm 126

The Tides That Turn

When God brought back the captives of Zion, we were like those who dream. Then our mouths were filled with laughter and our tongues with rejoicing.

Life is a turning tide, and I have experienced its highs and lows in relentless rhythm along many years and changes and moods. I know how the barrenness of the desert can be turned overnight into fertility *like the streams in the Negeb.* Sudden rains flood a dried-up riverbed, and all the fields along its course smile a spontaneous green. That is the power of the Lord's hand when it touches a parched land, or a human life.

Touch my life, Lord, release the streams of grace, turn the tide and make me smile for joy. And meanwhile give me the faith and the patience to wait for your time, with the certainty that the day will come and the streams will run again in the dry south.

I know the law of life: *May those who sow in tears reap with songs of joy!* Let me work and toil and struggle with the hope that one day the tide will turn and I will smile and sing. Let me realize that there is no success without hard work, no advancement without painstaking effort. For any progress in the life of my profession or of my spirit I must strain myself, bring out all my resources, do my best. The work of the sower is slow and taxing, but it becomes bearable with the promise of the future crop. I know that to reap I have to sow and to sing I have to weep first.

Is not my whole life a field to be sown in tears? I don't want to dramatize my existence, but there are enough tears in my life to justify the thought. Life is hard work, and sowing eternity is an uphill task. I pray that the certainty of the crop may already bring now a smile to my tired face. I ask to be allowed to borrow a song from the feast of heaven to practice it now with anticipated joy while I sow on earth.

Those that go forth weeping, carrying the seed for sowing, shall come home with shouts of joy, bringing the sheaves with them.

Psalm 127

Prayer of the Compulsive Worker

In vain you rise early and delay going to bed, toiling to make a living, since Yahweh provides for the beloved as they sleep.

Thank you, Lord, for this timely reminder. I work too much; I work because I believe myself to be indispensable; I work to achieve recognition; I work to escape from facing myself. And I cover up all that by saying that I work for you and your Kingdom and my brothers and sisters in it. Hard work for me is an addiction except it has a respectable name, and so I can be proud of it while I drug myself with its intoxication. I feel glad, Lord, that you have found me out and have plainly denounced my vice and declared its futility. You have gently laughed at my long hours of work and have with one word destroyed my reputation. Between you and me, Lord, I am happy you uncovered my plot, and I feel relieved of a burden I had uselessly put on my shoulders.

If Yahweh does not build the house, in vain do the builders toil; if Yahweh does not guard the city, in vain do the sentries watch.

Not that I don't have to work; I have to be at my desk just as the guard has to be at the gate if the city is to be protected. But in reality, Lord, you are watching the city, you are building the house, and you are doing the work at my desk. And your presence makes me feel lighter as we share responsibilities and I gently let the burden shift on to you.

I may still get up early, as a long habit is not easily broken, but I'll surely approach my work now with a light heart and a knowing smile. Let's pretend, let's keep up the show; let's play the game. Yes, work is only a game, and I now see it so and want to take it for what it is. No longer will I slog along for results, but will play a friendly match without worrying about the score. I already feel lighter and relaxed, closer to you, Lord, and even happier with my work. Do you know what I guess? I guess that now that I relax the grip on my work and reduce its time and its intensity, it's going to go even better!

Psalm 128

The Family Meal

It is a grace to take meals together, to sit at table with my brothers and sisters, to eat in common the fruit of our own labors, to feel like a family and talk and comment on the events of the day with the informal intimacy of a happy group. It is a blessing to have meals together. It may be that the common dining room unites us as much as the common chapel does. We are body and soul, and if we learn to pray together and to eat together we'll be halfway toward learning the necessary art of living together.

I want to learn the art of conversation at table, which frames a savory dish in the elegant gesture of wit and pleasantry. No business meals, no hurried lunches, no makeshift sandwiches at the office while work goes on: that is insulting the mind and trespassing on the body. A meal has its liturgy too, and I want to follow its rubrics with the reverence due to my body, which is a privileged part of God's creation.

Good food is a biblical blessing on a good person's table. I appreciate good food with Christian thanksgiving. It enlivens the most earthly part of our existence with the simplest of pleasures in its daily recurrence. Has not heaven been compared to a banquet by people who knew about it? If heaven is a banquet, every meal is a rehearsal for heaven.

May the psalm's blessing descend on all our meals as we say grace at table:

You will eat the fruit of your labor. Happy shall you be and prosperous.... May Yahweh bless you from Zion all the days of your life! May you see your children's children in a happy Jerusalem! Peace be upon Israel.

Psalm 129

My Enemies

It is hard for me to admit it even to myself, but it is a fact I can ignore no longer, and I'd better confess it to myself: I have enemies. There are people who dislike me, people who oppose me, people who try to hinder my work and ruin my successes. There are people who speak ill of me behind my back, who rejoice when I fail and feel sorry when I succeed. This is no persecution complex but the clear and simple admission of unpleasant reality. I am not everybody's friend, and it is good for me to know it.

They oppressed me from my youth, yet they have not destroyed me. Upon my back they have plowed; they make their furrows long.

The image is brutal, but the reality is no less inhuman. They plowed my back as a farmer plows the field with an iron blade. I wear the scars of enmity on the tissues of my soul. I want to accept the reality of my sufferings at other peoples' hands without myself bearing enmity or feeling embittered by the behavior against me of people I call my brothers and sisters.

My reflection today is not about them but about myself. The fact that I have enemies humbles me. I thought I was a fine person, attractive, and lovable to all. I realize it is not so. I don't blame anybody and don't blame myself but take notice of the blunt fact that chastens me: not everybody likes me.

My reaction now is that I can learn more about myself from my enemies than from my friends. Those who like me flatter me with their affection and their appreciation, while those who dislike me reveal my weak points to me with their criticism and their attacks. If I pay attention to the hidden messages behind the opposition I encounter, I can learn more about myself than in many hours of self-examination.

Self-knowledge is precious, and my opposers are the best source I can get it from. Without seeking to justify a situation I have to endure, I want now to draw from it the benefit of a rare gift for my soul. I want to grow in self-knowledge by studying the reactions I provoke in others, not only the favorable ones from my friends, but, and particularly so, the unfavorable ones from my enemies.

Thank you for those who oppose me, Lord. They are helping me to uncover my own true self.

Psalm 130

Prayer of Prayers

Out of the depths I cry to you, O God.

Whatever prayers I am making to you, Lord, I mean all of them to be preceded by this verse: *Out of the depths.* Whatever prayer I make to you, I mean, Lord. I make my prayer from the depths of my humility and from the depths of my heart; I make it from the seriousness of my experience and the urgency of my salvation. Whatever I pray, I pray with all my heart and all my soul, putting my whole life into each word, my whole being into every request. Every prayer I make is the breath of my soul, my hope of survival, and my claim to eternal joy. I am serious when I pray, Lord, and it is no routine, no habit, no need to conform to usage or keep appearances or be a good example that drives me to your presence and sets me on my knees. I need to be myself, in all the poverty of my being and all the greatness of my hope; and I can be that only before you in prayer. That is why I pray, Lord.

I know my misery. I know my indignity. I know my sin. But I also know your pardon and your grace, and I wait for you eagerly to receive your visit in time of need. *Out of the depths.*

My soul waits for you, O God. More than sentinels wait for the dawn.

Sense, Lord, my eagerness, and see my seriousness. I need you as the night watch needs the dawn. I need you as the earth needs the sun. When I pray, I pray in dead earnest, knowing as I do that you are everything to me, and that prayer is my daily link with you.

So today I pray for my prayers. I remind myself before you of their meaning and their importance. I pray to continue to pray from the depth of my heart, and I pray for you to continue to see each of my prayers as a prayer of my whole being for my whole life.

Out of the depths I cry to you, O God.

Psalm 131

The Prayer of the Intellectual

Too many words, Lord, too many ideas, too many arguments. Even to my prayer have I brought the weight of my own reasoning—the irrational burden of my rationality. I am an addict of the syllogism, a slave of reason, a victim of enlightenment. I cloud my prayers with my sophistication and blunt the edge of my needs with the verbosity of my expressions. I have seen my vice, and I want to return for once to the simplicity and the innocence of childhood. I feel happy to do so.

Yahweh, my heart has no false pride; my eyes do not look too high. I am not concerned with great affairs or things far above me. It is enough for me to keep my soul still and quiet like a child in its mother's arms, as content as a child that has been weaned.

I submit myself, Lord. I submit my intellect to you. I put aside my concepts, my knowledge, my theories, my lucubrations. I have thought so much that I have made the intellect you gave me to find you into an obstacle to seeing you. I submit, Lord. Tame my reason, and chasten my thought. Still my intellect, and pacify my mind. Suppress the noise within me that does not allow me to hear your voice in my heart.

Let me rest in your arms, O Lord, like a child in its mother's arms. How much I love that image! I close my eyes; I relax my limbs; I feel the gentle touch, the warmth, the care. I fall asleep in the simplicity of my soul. This is the prayer that does me most good, Lord.

Psalm 132

A Dwelling for the Lord

David had a noble heart. He had his failings, too, but redeemed the impulses of his passion with the nobility of his reactions. He could not bear that the Ark of the Lord rested yet under a tent while he had a king's palace in the newly conquered Jerusalem. His reaction when he realized this was typical of him:

I will not enter my house or go to the bed where I rest. I will give no sleep to my eyes; to my eyelids I will give no slumber until I find a place for God, a dwelling for the Mighty One of Israel.

Since then the obsession of Israel was to find a worthy *resting-place* for the Ark they had brought through the desert as witness and instrument of God's presence with them.

Arise, Yahweh, and come to the place of your rest, you and the ark of your strength. The Lord accepted the invitation of his people, and chose Zion for his home: *"This is my resting-place forever, here I have chosen to live."*

A *resting-place* for the Lord. Glory and pride of Israel. If the first commandment is to love the Lord above all things, a practical consequence of it will be to prepare for him a building above all buildings. Such a faith has given rise to the most beautiful manifestations of the art and imagination of humankind, whose zeal and endeavor have covered all the corners of inhabited earth with temples. The most majestic dwellings today on earth are your temples, Lord, and we who believe feel in our hearts the satisfaction David felt when he pronounced his oath. You have a worthy *resting-place* on earth, Lord.

Our uneasiness now is rather the opposite, Lord. You have now a *resting-place*, but many people do not. Today many of your children do not have roofs over their heads to protect them from heat and cold, from wind and rain. David's oath hangs heavily over our heads in this new dimension that our consciences open for us. How can I sleep in a comfortable bed when my brothers and sisters sleep in the street under a ruthless sky? How can I build a house of cedar for myself when the Ark of the Lord, the poor of the Lord, live in huts whose walls are newspapers and whose roofs are made of plastic bags heaped together?

Whatever we do to the smallest of human beings, we do to you, Lord. To find habitable dwellings for these, your children, is to find dwellings for you. I renew David's oath in the name of all humankind and pray that you may not allow us to rest in sinful complacency while our brothers and sisters suffer the naked scourge of weather in a homeless existence.

O God, remember David and all the many hardships he endured, the oath he swore to Yahweh, his vow to the Mighty One of Jacob.

Psalm 133

Family Prayer

The greatest blessing in a home is that all brothers and sisters in it love one another. In the many years they live together they learn to play together, to fight together, to know one another as no one else ever will know them, to defend one another with a loyalty unequaled by any other loyalty on earth: the loyalty of members of one family. Blood speaks in humankind, and brothers and sisters have the same blood running in their veins.

How good it is and how pleasant, for God's people to live in unity.

One may add, with the sadness of experience and the realism of history, "—and how rare!" The strongest bonds of nature can be loosened, and the very witness of the one blood can be silenced. Kindred persecutes kindred, and the pages of history are stained with the records of wars among families. Peace in a home is no obvious atmosphere to be taken for granted but a noble achievement to be strived after with common determination by all.

A special blessing from the Lord awaits that happy family achievement. The fragrance of oil and the freshness of dew will signify the smoothness and richness of life together. Unity is strength, and unity is happiness in the family where all members live together in harmony.

I pray for each family, I pray for mine, I pray for all brothers and sisters in the world, that familial love may fully occupy its beneficent place in the hearts of all people.

For there Yahweh has promised a blessing, life that never ends.

Psalm 134

Vigils in the Night

You made the night for rest, Lord, but many people do not find rest in their nights. Some have to work at night; some travel; some study; some watch; some turn in their beds while sleep eludes their tired souls. I pray with all the victims of the night, with all those who are awake while darkness covers the earth and invites them to a rest that is not theirs to enjoy.

I remember you in the vigils of the night. I unite myself in sleepless kinship with those who stay awake to pronounce your name, to contemplate your truth, to watch your Temple, to continue during the night the sacrifice of praise others offer in the day, so that no hour may remain without the sweet odor of prayer in the presence of your ever-watching majesty.

Come, bless Yahweh, all you who serve Yahweh, ministering in the house of Yahweh! . . . Lift up your hands toward the sanctuary; praise Yahweh night after night!

Teach me, Lord, how to bless you during the day and during the night, in wakefulness and slumber, in light and in darkness, in work and in leisure. Teach me to sanctify my nights with the memory of your name. Make me thus worthy to receive the blessing of the priests who keep vigil in your holy Temple, proclaiming you Lord of the day and of the night with their presence.

May Yahweh bless you from Zion, the One who made heaven and earth! Bless my nights, O Lord, as you bless my days!

Psalm 135

Og and Sihon

Og and Sihon—names in the history of Israel, which is my own history. Og and Sihon. The kings that would not let Israel pass. Giants among mortals, conceited in their power, men who denied right of way to the Israelites even when the Israelites promised not to touch their vineyards or drink from their wells, obstacles on the way to the Promised Land. God laid them low with all their people. The Lord will not tolerate that anything or anybody try to stop the forward march of his People toward their destiny. Israel will remember those foreign names and make them symbol and memory of timely deliverance against impossible odds, a legend in its annals and a verse in the psalms of thanksgiving for help and victory.

Obstacles on the way to the Promised Land. Og and Sihon are also present in my memory, dangers I have experienced, disappointments I have met, moments when it seemed all chances were over, or mistakes that appeared to invalidate any effort to go ahead. My own way to spiritual progress seems to have been blocked, more times than I care to remember, by unyielding obstacles that marked almost the end of the journey, my own enemies like giant kings and proud armies. On my part, there was spiritual fatigue and lack of faith. How could I get by? How could I go ahead?

Yet those unsurmountable obstacles disappeared; the way was cleared, and the journey continued. A mighty hand opened the way for me again and renewed hopes and bestowed courage. I have my own legends and my own names too, my own private memories and my own secret history. No more obstacles, however formidable, will now frighten me. So long as I remember Og and Sihon, my way will remain open till the end.

Yahweh struck down nations in their greatness, and God slew mighty rulers: Sihon, king of the Amorites, Og, the king of Bashan, and all the kings of Canaan. Yahweh gave Israel their land as an inheritance, an inheritance for God's people. Yahweh, your name stands forever, remembered from age to age.

Psalm 136

The Great Hallel

We give thanks to you, Yahweh, for you are good. Your love is everlasting! We give thanks to you, God of gods. Your love is everlasting! Give thanks to the God of heaven, for God's love is everlasting!

Israel sings its thanksgiving in the feast of the Pasch, listing with loving memory all the great works of the Lord, from creation and deliverance to conquest and daily care, under the meaningful monotony of the single refrain: *Your love is everlasting!*

Your wisdom made the heavens. Your love is everlasting! You spread out the earth on the waters. Your love is everlasting! You made the great lights. Your love is everlasting! The sun to rule the day. Your love is everlasting! The moon and stars to rule the night. Your love is everlasting!

To the official litany I add my own private verses.

You brought me to life. Your love is everlasting! You placed me in a loving family. Your love is everlasting! You taught me to pronounce your name. Your love is everlasting! You opened your Scriptures to me. Your love is everlasting! You called me to your service. Your love is everlasting! You sent me to help your people. Your love is everlasting! You give joy in my heart. Your love is everlasting! You have called me your friend. Your love is everlasting!

Now I go on in the silence of my heart, recounting those moments that God and I alone know, moments of bliss and intimacy, moments of sorrow and repentance, moments of mercy and grace. His love is everlasting.

I think of my life as made into a prayer, my memories into a loving litany, my history into a psalm. And after every event, big or small, painful or delightful, hidden or manifest, comes the verse that gives meaning to all and unifies my life in the single thrust of God's own providence: His love is everlasting.

We give thanks to you, Yahweh, for you are good. Your love is everlasting!

Psalm 137

How Can I Sing?

How could we sing a song of Yahweh while in a foreign land?

This is the cross and paradox of my own life, Lord. How can I sing when others weep? How can I dance when others mourn? How can I eat when others starve? How can I sleep when others watch? How can I rest when others toil? How can I live when others die? This world is exile, trial, and contradiction. How can I speak of happiness in it when I see misery all around me and in my own soul?

Rivers invite gaity, but we weep by their side; trees wave their branches to music, but we have hung our mute harps on them; people ask for songs, but we answer with laments. How can we speak of Jerusalem while we are in Babylon!

By the rivers of Babylon we sat and wept, remembering Zion. On the poplars of that land we hung up our harps; there our captors asked of us the lyrics of our songs and urged us to be joyous: "Sing for us one of the songs of Zion!" they said. How could we sing a song of Yahweh while in a foreign land?

Make me sensitive, Lord, to the pain around me. Do not allow me to forget the sufferings of human beings far and near, the trials of humankind in our age, the agony of millions in the face of hunger, destitution, and death. Let me not grow callous, forgetful, or deaf. Human beings suffer, and life is exile. Those who suffer are my brothers and sisters, and I suffer with them.

There is a time for joy in life, but there is also the serious, tragic consciousness of the plight of our age and our responsibility to alleviate suffering and restore peace.

I want to sing, Lord, to sing the praises of your name and the joys of life as you taught me in the festivals of Zion. But I cannot sing now in the bitterness of exile. Thus my very negative, "How can I sing?" is a prayer to you that you may shorten the exile, redeem humankind, and bring joy back to earth that I may sing again.

If you want to hear again the songs of Zion, Lord, bring the joy of Zion back on the face of the earth.

Psalm 138

Do Not Leave Unfinished
the Work of Your Hands!

*You will do everything you have promised me; Yahweh, your
faithful love endures forever. Complete the work that you have begun.*

I find those words most consoling for me at this moment,
Lord. *You will do everything you have promised me.* I know that you
have a purpose for me. I know that you have begun your work in
me, and I know that you bring to completion what you begin. In
that thought I rest. I am in good hands. The work is on. It will not
stop midway. You are sure to complete it. Thank you, Lord.

You yourself spoke with condemnation of those who begin
and do not end, of the plower who looks back at the middle of the
furrow, of the builder who stops building at the middle of the
tower. That means that you are not like that, Lord. You drive the
furrow till the end; you finish the tower; you complete your work.
And I am your work. Your hands have made me, and your grace
has brought me where I am. Don't disclaim responsibility, Lord.
Don't leave me in the lurch. Don't disown your work. Your own
reputation is at stake. Do not let people, when they see me, say of
you: "He began to build and did not finish the work." Bring to a
happy ending what you have begun in me, Lord.

You have given me the desires; give me now the execution of
those desires. You have invited me to take vows; give me now the
strength to keep them. You have inspired me to start on my way
to you; give me now the determination to arrive. Why did you call
me, if you were not going to follow up your first call with conse-
quent graces to ensure continuance and success? If you were
going to drop me along the way, why did you in the first instance
hold my hand?

I am in the midst of my way, and I feel the difficulty, the doubt, the fatigue. That is why today it is a great consolation to me to think of your seriousness, your commitment, your promise. *You will do everything you have promised me.* That gives me hope when my strength fails and courage when my faith begins to falter. I may fail, but you will not. You have committed yourself to me. And you will carry out your commitment to the end.

Allow me now to express my faith in a prayer, my firm conviction as a humble request in words that you have given me and that I love to pronounce: *Complete the work that you have begun.*

Psalm 139

You Know Me
Through and Through

Yahweh, you search me and know me. You know if I am standing or sitting. You perceive my thoughts from far away. Whether I walk or lie down, you are watching; you are familiar with all my ways. Before a word is even on my tongue, Yahweh, you know it completely. . . . Such knowledge is beyond my understanding, too high beyond my reach.

You know my thoughts, my words, my going and coming, my motives and passions, my loyalty and my failings, my character, my personality. You know me better than I know myself. You understand me when I don't understand myself. I am relieved to know that there is at least someone who understands me!

I know that self-knowledge is the way to mental health and to spiritual realization. I have strived for that self-knowledge without success, and now I realize that it is in you that I can find myself, in your mirror that I can see my face, in your knowledge of me that I can find self-knowledge. Dealing with you in prayer will lead me to know myself. I feel happy to have realized that.

You know even my body, which, I begin to realize now, plays a much more important part in my life than I had ever suspected, being united with my soul in intimate unity, mutual influence, and integrated being.

You created my inmost being and knit me together in my mother's womb. . . . You know me through and through from having watched my bones take shape when I was being formed in secret, woven together in the womb. You have seen my every action; all were recorded in your book—my days determined even before the first one began. God, your thoughts are mysterious!

Lead me day by day to understand my body as you understand it. Make me appreciate the wonder of your creation and love the gift of matter in my being. Reconcile me with my materiality, and make me feel proud of my contact with earth through the clay of my body.

Make me love my senses, trust their wisdom, follow their insights. Make me feel one with nature through them and establish a kinship of seeing, hearing, and tasting with all the material world you have created to keep me company on my way to you.

And then lead me to understand the whole of me, soul and body, mind and senses, wisdom and folly, in the uniqueness of my character and the sacredness of my nature that bears your seal. Give me, Lord, the supreme grace of self-knowledge face-to-face with you in the context of your creation.

You know me through and through, Lord. Make me know myself!

Psalm 140

Justice to the Downtrodden

I know that God secures justice for the poor and upholds the cause
of the needy.

I renew my faith in your justice, Lord, in the face of a world
where justice seems to fail. I have tried prayers and action; I have
tried words and writings; I have tried persuasion and revolution,
and yet injustice continues to thrive on the face of the earth. What
more can I do?

I cannot sit down in resignation and leave things as they are,
and I can do nothing to change them despite all my efforts. I long
for a just world with all my heart, but I see glaring injustice all
around me. I believe in a just God, but I live in an unjust society. I
suffer, Lord, and I want you to know it.

I know that your views are different from mine, that you see
what I do not see and that your time is measured in eternity. But
my life is finite, Lord, and I expect to get a glimpse of your justice
while I walk on your earth.

I know that human happiness is deceptive and that riches
may bring misery while poverty may bring joy. But my spirit
revolts before inhuman degradation, and my heart cannot stand
the look of hunger on the face of a child.

I don't want to preach; I don't want to argue; I don't want to
pray. I want to be one with the suffering of my brothers and
sisters to remind you, in the unity of existence and faith, of the
plight of your people on earth.

Psalm 141

The Evening Sacrifice

My prayers rise like incense, my hands like the evening sacrifice.

It is evening, Lord. The day has passed with its flurry of activity, meetings, work, people listening and talking, papers and letters, and decisions and doubts. I don't even quite know what I have done and what I have said, but the day is over and I want to offer it to you, Lord, just as it was, before I close the account and turn the page.

Take this day as an incense stick that has burned before you hour by hour while it left in the ashes of the past the fragrance of its present. Take it as my raised hands, symbol and instrument of my actions to live my life and establish your Kingdom. Take it as an evening sacrifice that enacts on the altar of time the liturgy of eternity. Take it as my prayer, Lord, which is my faith, my commitment, and my life. Accept at the end of the day the homage of my earthly existence.

I don't justify my actions; I don't defend my decisions; I don't excuse my failings; I just place my day before you as it has been, as I have lived it, as you have seen it. Take it in your gaze and file it away in the folds or your mercy. Its memory is safe with you, and I can now let go of it with easy confidence. Relieve me of the burden of this day, that it may not haunt my memory or wound my thoughts. Wipe its regrets clean from my mind so that no mental residue may hurt me, no remainder weigh on my conscience. Like the streak of incense, it has burnt itself out and now dissolves into perfume, slowly vanishing into nothingness, filling the space around with the elusive touch of its invisible presence, while leaving no trace of guilt, worry, expectation, or attachment on my open soul.

Accept my evening sacrifice, Lord. Heal my memories and close my past, that I may live in fullness the blessing of the present.

Psalm 142

I Cry Aloud

I have prayed in my mind, and I have prayed in a group; I have prayed in silence, and I have prayed in a soft voice. Today I pray aloud; I lift my voice; I shout in public. I want to try all ways of reaching you, Lord, as my moods lead me and the presence of my brothers and sisters inspires me. In any case I am using the words you put in my mouth, Lord.

With all my voice I cry to you, Yahweh; with all my voice I entreat you.

My cry speaks my urgency even without the meaning of words. I need not specify my petitions or spell out my expectations. You know my needs, and I don't want to worry you with the details. I only want attention. I want you to listen to my cry in the presence of your people. I want to remind you of my existence. I want to break the silence of complacency with the shamelessness of my cry. Let people turn their heads and wonder. I am in pain, and I shout it out before you. Let my pain reach you in my cry.

My pain is not for me, but for my brothers and sisters, my friends, the poor, and the oppressed—for all those who suffer and all those who toil under the pressure of injustice and the harshness of life. My cry is the cry of suffering humanity, all voices united in one, because suffering levels out high and low in the kinship of a common sorrow. For all of them I cry with the sharpness of my own agony and the echo of humankind's sufferings in this valley of tears.

I cry to you, Yahweh. . . . Listen, then, to my cry, for I am in the depths of distress.

Psalm 143

In the Morning

At dawn remind me of your faithful love. . . . You are my God— teach me to do your will.

I wake up, and my eyes lift to you. My first thought flies to your side at the beginning of a new day. I don't know what awaits me; I haven't yet planned my day or fixed my work. Before any other thought comes I want to contact you for your blessing and your smile as life opens again on the world and on me. Good morning, Lord, and may this day keep me close to you.

The morning is the time of prayer and worship, the renewal of the promise of life with the first ray of light, the propitious time when you, Lord, come to the help of your people. In the morning I stand before you to receive anew the gift of life in continued creation. Your gift is your way to let me experience your true love as I face life again. I will always need your love, Lord.

The one prayer I make to lead my day is: *Teach me to do your will.* I know the day will bring choices and decisions, doubts and temptations, darkness and trials. My one concern in all this as I begin the daily journey is to know your will and do it at each moment. My day will be truly mine when it is fully yours. My decisions will be correct when they carry out your will. My journey will be straight when you are its aim. Your will is the advance summary of my day, and to discover it step by step is my task and my joy.

Give me light, like the rays of the sun that begin to filter shyly through the curtains of my window. Give me joy like the birds that begin to sing to wake up all nature on time. Give me faith like the flowers that open their petals to the breeze with friendly trust. Give me strength; give me love; give me life.

I trust in you—at dawn remind me of your faithful love.

Psalm 144

What Are Human Beings?

God, what are we, that you care for us or even take thought of us? We are like a breath, our days, like a passing shadow.

I am not saying this in a fit of depression; I am not voicing a complaint, much less disparaging myself. I only want to put my life in its proper perspective, reduce things to size, and learn to take myself lightly. I understand this to be a healthy approach to a happy life, and I want you to help me in this endeavor, Lord.

Yes, I am a puff of wind and a passing shadow. Such a thought reduces the volume of my problems and takes away the ground from under the throne of my self-importance. What can be lighter and happier than a puff of wind and a passing shadow? I will enjoy things all the more when they don't stick to me and move more swiftly through life once its burden is made light. It is not for me to solve all the world's problems and to right all the wrongs of modern society. I will move and will pass, doing my genuine best at each moment, but without the impossible seriousness of being the redeemer of all evils and the savior of humankind. I am not that. I am a puff of wind and a passing shadow. Let me pass and let me fly, and let my fleeting presence bring a moment of relief to those it touches, a gesture of goodwill in a world heavy with sorrow.

Light and happy. I am a puff of wind, but that wind is the wind of your Spirit, Lord. I am a passing shadow, but that shadow is cast by the pillar of cloud that leads your People through the desert. I am your shadow, and I am your breeze. That is the happiest definition of my humble life. Thank you for it, Lord.

Happy the people for whom this is true; happy the people whose God is Yahweh.

Psalm 145

Generation to Generation

I often think of the generation gap. Today when I contemplate the history of your People, their traditions, their public prayer, and their singing of psalms together, I think rather of the generation link. One generation instructs the other; they hand down their beliefs and their practices; they pray together, uniting young and old voices in a concert of continuity through the sands of the desert of life.

Generation after generation praises your work and proclaims your might.

The subject of Israel's prayer is its own history, and thus while praying they preserve their heritage and learn it anew, shaping the mind of the young as they recite the common psalmody with the old, creating a chorus of unity in a world of discord.

I love your psalms, Lord, above any other prayer because of this unification. I thank you for these psalms; I treasure them, and by using them day after day I want to enter deeper into my own history as a member of your People and to learn to communicate this history to the brothers and sisters who come after me.

They discourse on the power of your wonderful deeds and declare your greatness. They publish the fame of your abundant goodness and joyfully sing of your justice.

Make the praying of your psalms a bond of unity in your People, Lord!

Psalm 146

No Subservience to Others

Do not put your trust in rulers.

This is a timely admonition, which I adapt to my life and my circumstances: Do not depend on others. I am not thinking of the healthy cooperation in which one helps another, as we all need one another to stand together in the common task of living. I am thinking of inner dependence, of needing the approval of others, of being swayed by public opinion, of becoming a plaything of the likes and dislikes of those around us, of courting the favor of *rulers*. There are no *rulers* in my life, no dependence on the whims of others, no subservience to humanity.

I am accountable only to you, Lord. It is your judgment that matters to me and no one else's. I don't give anyone the right to judge me. I am my own judge because my conscience reflects the sentence of your supreme court in the capacity of my honesty. I am no better when anybody praises me and no worse when somebody derides me. I refuse to feel low when I hear people speak ill of me, and I decline to feel elated when they extol me to the skies. I know my worth, and I know my smallness. No human judge will judge me.

This is my freedom; this is my right to be myself; this is my happiness as a person. My life is on my conscience, and my conscience is in your hands. You alone are my Ruler, Lord.

Happy those whose help is the God of Jacob and Rachel, whose hope is in Yahweh, their God.

Psalm 147a

Of Hearts and Stars

God heals the brokenhearted and binds up all their wounds. God knows the number of the stars and calls them each by name.

Your power, O Lord, extends from the human heart to the stars in heaven. You are the Lord of humanity and the Lord of creation, and I like to proclaim the two realms of your majesty in a single verse, to encompass in one gesture the whole expanse of your vast domain. The beatings of the human heart and the orbits of heavenly bodies, human behavior and heavenly trajectories, conscience and space are all in your hand, and I rejoice when I think of it.

If you know how to handle the stars, will you now know also how to handle my heart? Please, Lord, take it in hand. Its orbit is rather crazy, it is not easy to know today what it will do tomorrow—when it will fly at a tangent and when it will refuse to move in stubborn emptiness. Ease it gently into regular orbit, Lord; watch its path and tend its course with heavenly care and calculated firmness. Let it be a star to enliven the night sky over the world of mortals.

I relax, Lord, in your power and your wisdom. The sky is my home, and I roam happily in the vastness of your creation under your loving gaze. Call me by my name, Lord, as you call the stars in heaven and your children on earth. Call me by my name, as the shepherd calls his sheep. I am happy to know that you know my name. Use it freely, Lord, to call me to order and to joy whenever you want. And one day, Lord, use my name to call me by your side forever.

Great is our God and mighty in power; there is no limit to God's wisdom.

Psalm 147b

Winter Song

God sends forth a command to the earth; swiftly runs the word! God spreads snow like wool and scatters frost like ashes. God scattters hail like crumbs; before God's cold, the waters freeze. God sends a word and melts them; God lets the breeze blow and the waters flow.

The soft snow speaks silence on the winter scene. Snow—white grace from heaven to cover the earth. The recess of winter slows down the race of life, and there is a promise in the water on the frozen fields when the snow melts with the early warmth of spring. Thank you for the snow, Lord.

Your power is hidden, Lord, in the gentle flakes that land softly over trees and land. No sound, no pressure, no violence, and yet everything yields to the invisible hand of the master painter. See your action, Lord, gentle and powerful over the human heart.

Your power is universal, Lord. Nothing escapes your influence on the whole wide earth. The whole landscape is white. You reach the high mountains and the low valleys. You cover the closed cities and the open fields. You touch the heart of the wise and the simple. You love the saint and the sinner. Your grace reaches all.

Your coming is unexpected, Lord. I wake up one morning and see the earth from my window suddenly turned white during the unsuspecting night. You know the time and the hour. You rule the seasons and the tides. At the right time you bring down the cooling blessing of your grace on the passions of my heart. Stop the fire, Lord, before I burn.

Lord of the sun and the stars, Lord of rain and storm, Lord of snow and ice, Lord of nature, which is your creation and my home, I rejoice when I see your action on earth, and I welcome with joy the material messengers that visit me from heaven as reminders of your love and assurance of your help.

Lord of the four seasons! I worship you in the temple of nature.

Psalm 148

Praise

Praise God from the heavens; praise God in the heights; praise God, all you angels; praise God, all you heavenly hosts. Praise God, sun and moon; praise God, all you shining stars. Praise God, you highest heavens, and you waters above the heavens. Let them praise the name of God, who commanded and they were created.

Praise is the language of heaven. Let us learn it on earth to practice for eternity.

Praise is the prayer of acceptance. We praise the Lord for things as they are, without presuming to improve them.

Praise is the prayer that makes contact. We do not escape into petition or complaint but assume reality into prayer.

Praise is the prayer of the present moment. It is not a pardon for the past nor protection for the future.

Praise is the prayer of the group—the choir of many voices before God's holy altar.

Praise is the prayer of joy. I cannot say "Praise the Lord!" with a gloomy face.

Praise is the prayer of love. Sincere praise rejoices because it loves the person it praises.

Praise is obedience—my status as creature put into music and song.

Praise is power. The walls of Jericho fall at the sound of the trumpets in the liturgy of the priests.

Praise is worship. Praise is dealing with God as God in the majesty of his glory.

Praise God all the earth, you sea monsters and all depths, fire and hail, snow and mist, storm winds that fulfill God's word. You mountains and all you hills, you fruit trees and all you cedars, you wild beasts and all tame animals, you creeping things and flying birds. Let the rulers of the earth and all peoples and all the judges of the earth—young men too, and maidens, old women and men—praise the name of God.

Psalm 149

Dance

Let Israel rejoice in their Maker; let the people of Zion be glad in their God. Let them praise God's name in a festive dance; let them sing praise to God with timbrel and harp.

I want to dance, in my mind if not with my body, to express with the totality of my being the totality of my submission to God. I want to dance, as David danced before the Ark, as Israel danced before the Temple, as all people have danced in religious worship of the Lord of spirit and matter.

Dance is the body made prayer, a psalm of gestures, a liturgy of movements. The body speaks better than the mind, and one gracious bow is worth a thousand contemplations. If singing is "praying twice," what will dancing be?

Dancing commits the dancer in the presence of the people. It is public and open and evident. A dance is a profession of faith. The dancer has a claim to a solemn promise: "If anyone acknowledges me before others, I will acknowledge that one before my Father in heaven."

Dancing brings art into prayer, and that noble adventure deserves gratitude from all men and women who love prayer and love art. Why should religious pictures be ugly? Why should religious books be dull? Why should prayer be boring? Why should faith be abstract? Dance changes all that with a swaying of the body and a clapping of the hands. Art and religion. Beauty and truth. I want to learn to make my prayer lively and my worship artistic for the joy of my heart and the glory of my God.

Let the faithful rejoice; let them sing for joy.

Psalm 150
Music

Praise to you, Yahweh, with the blast of the trumpet, praise with lyre and harp. Praise with timbrel and dance; praise with strings and flute. Praise to you, Yahweh, with resounding cymbals; praise with clanging cymbals. Let everything that has breath praise Yahweh. Alleluia.

Every time I listen to music, I think of you, Lord. Music is humankind's purest creation, and in it human beings come closest to you in the expression of their soul and the sublimeness of their art. Pure sound, wordless harmony, air made beauty, and space filled with joy. I wonder, while I listen to humankind's masterpieces, what divine touch of unearthly inspiration could have produced the thrill of sheer perfection that lifts the mind to regions not quite of this world. You are present to me, Lord, in the strings of a quartet or the chords of a symphony with a reality that touches sacramental grace in the uplifting consecration of my whole being. Thank you, Lord, for the gift of music in my life.

Praise the Lord with violins and violas, with cellos and double basses, with flutes and piccolos; praise him with pianos and harps, with harmoniums and organs, with mandolins and guitars; praise him with oboes and clarinets, with bassoons and tubas, with horns and trumpets; praise him with trombones and xylophones, with drums and timpani, with triangles and gongs. *Let everything that has breath praise Yahweh. Alleluia.*

Index of Prayer Themes

This index of prayer themes has been expanded from Father Valles's original in order to better serve the needs of the reader. It may be used as a reference for this book as well as for the Psalms in general. In order to promote this more general use, the psalm, rather than the page, numbers are given. Following the index is a list of Father Valles's favorite psalms.

Favorite Psalms of Father Valles

Psalm 2
Psalm 8
Psalm 14
Psalm 19
Psalm 22
Psalm 27
Psalm 30
Psalm 34
Psalm 37
Psalm 40
Psalm 42
Psalm 44
Psalm 45
Psalm 46
Psalm 55

Psalm 60
Psalm 63
Psalm 65
Psalm 67
Psalm 74
Psalm 78
Psalm 89
Psalm 95
Psalm 105
Psalms 114
& 115
Psalm 138
Psalm 144
Psalm 148
Psalm 149